GOD SENT ME BACK

GOD SENT ME BACK

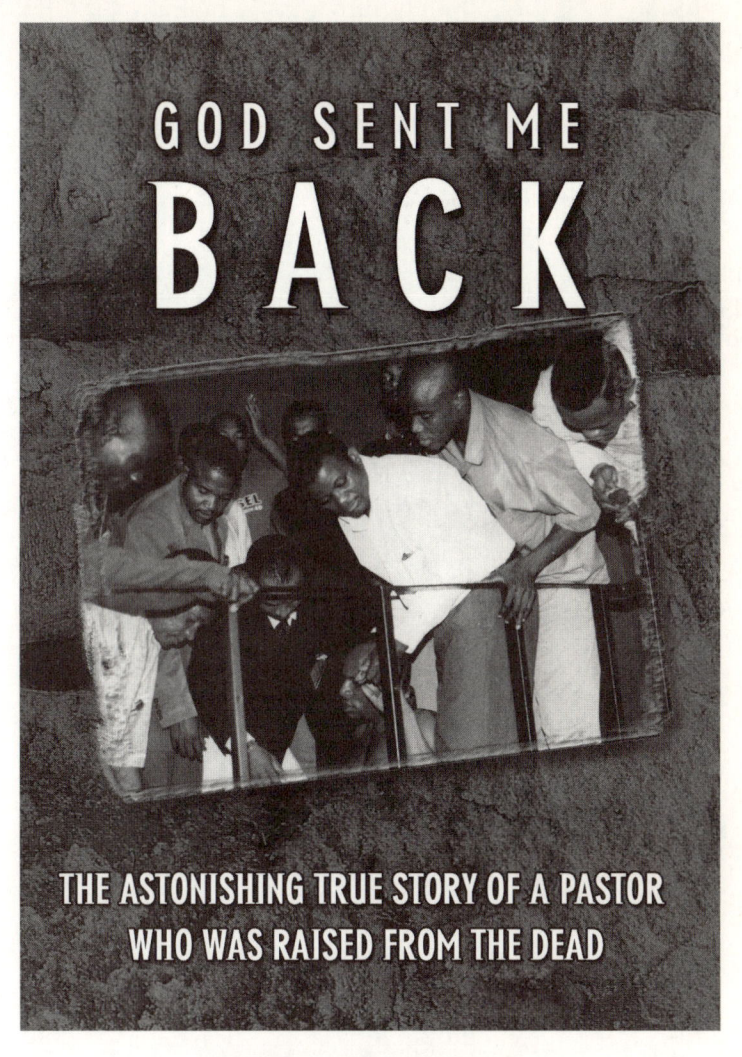

THE ASTONISHING TRUE STORY OF A PASTOR WHO WAS RAISED FROM THE DEAD

BISI DANIELS
with Isaac Achor

HighWay
A division of Anomalos Publishing House
Crane

HighWay
A division of Anomalos Publishing House, Crane 65633
© 2008 by Bisi Daniels with Isaac Achor
All rights reserved. Published 2008
Printed in the United States of America
08 1
ISBN-10: 0981764320 (paper)
EAN-13: 9780981764320 (paper)

Cover illustration and design by Steve Warner

A CIP catalog record for this book is available from the Library of Congress.

Contents

Preface ... vii

1. In the Beginning ... 1

2. In Ministry ... 19

3. The Accident ... 57

4. Nneka's Testimony ... 77

5. I Saw Heaven ... 93

6. To Heaven and Back ... 109

Quotes from Key Witnesses ... 115

Preface

God himself must have wanted this story told. How else could we explain the curious string of events that led to it? I was told about the subject of this book, Rev. Dan Ekechukwu— who I called "The Man Who Died," while I was writing *How I Was Called* (a book on how notable Nigerian pastors were called into ministry).

Interviewing "The Man Who Died" a week later for *How I Was Called* seemed like pulling the plug on a story rich enough to merit its own book. The story involved a man whom God handpicked from the rot to bless. Well, God chooses whom to bless, and, in many cases, his reasons defy logic.

However, writing a story that risks putting one's reputation on the line and the effrontery of investigating God, called for caution.

Nonetheless, two days of heated editorial debate unveiled an equally powerful attraction. Rev. Dan Ekechukwu was raised from the dead at a function presided over by renowned Evangelist Reinhard Bonnke. This fact could represent God's way of giving the miracle an international appeal. Of course, if the had incident happened in the remote village of Amaimo, it would have raised doubts strong enough to kill the story.

My colleague, Isaac, and I set out to interview (in their Ikeja office) Rev. Dan Ekechukwu and his wife Nneka for the book. During interviews that lasted more than three days, we discovered a thread of truth worth investigating: Dan isn't ashamed to reveal the poverty and sin-infested life from which God called him to service. Nneka was honest about her pain over how her own relations contributed to Dan's horrific beginning as a man of God. She revealed how her in-laws had locked her out of all the property she shared with Dan in Onitsha upon hisdeath. These were both compelling leads. For one thing, the in-laws would not have attempted what they did, even in defiance of the opposition of the church elders, if they were not convinced their son was dead. Encouraged by these deductions, we set out to explore all the settings of the miracle. There was undeniable proof of the accident at St. Charles Borromeo Hospital in Onitsha where he was first taken but prematurely discharged at the insistance of his wife. The hospital corroborated the fact that he had been admitted. They even admitted the controversy of having to discharge a patient in such a terrible state of health to his wife, who wanted him out of the hospital.

That also raised a big question. Why did Nneka subject Dan, who was in such an awful state, to a bumpy two-hour ride to an Owerri hospital? This was same hospital where Dan had previously been saved from the cold hands of death after a robbery attack masterminded by his blood brother. However, we were encouraged by the fact that human errors sometimes serve as scenes in God's drama of miracles.

The Umezurike Hospital in Owerri verified that Dan was a patient. The story was also confirmed at St. Eunice Clinic in Owerri where Dan was finally confirmed dead.

Witnesses at Amaimo, including his parents, told a consistent story. The body language of his mother, Mabel, who was forced to raise a sickly Dan, revealed a clear sign of triumph over pain. Now a proud mother, she smiles infectiously. Another convincing piece of evidence was discovered at the Ikeduru Community Hospital mortuary. Both the official records of the dead and the mortician told the same story.

Upon returning to Onitsha to continue our investigation, we found the bustling commercial town in a dire mood. A heavy downpour had flooded all the neglected streets, and our car swam like an amphibious automobile. Despite this, we waded through the muddy waters, sometimes pushing the car through water that had risen to waist level.

Luckily, we found Oyibo Okechukwu, pastor of the church Dan first attended after God reached down to lift him from the rot. He knew Dan very well, and he had no doubt about the miracle. We visited many other places, and spoke with other people who were relevant to the story.

One man we happened to miss was Reverend Dr. Paul Nwachukwu. Twice we visited, and twice we missed him. However, his magnificent hilltop church revealed ample evidence of Bonnke's presence on the day of the miracle. Some of the church members we met confirmed the story with pride. We were also fortunate to find his verbal evidence on various tapes for which we have to thank the church.

Even with the wealth of evidence, we subjected the story to the scrutiny of reasonable third parties. They included: Yvette Moyse of London and Andrew Masade, a veteran journalist, writer and critic in Lagos who both edited parts of the story; "Edit 9ll" editor, Marc Baldwin and a tenured professor of English in Tampa, Florida who edited the manuscript quickly because he found the document "very inspirational."

PREFACE

Photographer and journalist, Aoiri Obaigbo, queried the story at every point of the investigation to ensure we were not misled.

To preserve the inspiration of the story, I wrote in the first person.

Bisi Daniels

one

In the Beginning

Although I was a pastor for eight years and am now an evangelist, I still find it difficult to adequately explain God's special love for me. Every chapter in my 33-year-old life has been a miracle. In fact, I have experienced so many miracles that today, when I look back, I see the glittering sheet of God's glory spread over the grime and uncertainty of my past life. Even when I strayed from the paths of righteousness, the splendour of God's grace shone through the utter darkness.

Poverty forced me out of school at the age of twelve, when I was in primary three. As a result, I could not speak good English when I started dawn street preaching. I preached in Igbo. When my interpreter abandoned me, I prayed for support. The following morning, when God touched my lips, I started preaching in English on the streets of Onitsha in Eastern Nigeria. I have continued to preach in English ever since.

I was taken to a stream to be killed by ritualists who blamed Christianity for their dwindling patronage. However, I walked back home, thanks to Divine Intervention.

When I was a pastor of a flourishing church, my blood brother and several armed robbers attacked me and slit my throat. I survived the attack and continued my ministry.

Then I was killed in an automobile accident. After three days, I was raised miraculously from the dead to tell my story and spread the great Truth of the glory of the Kingdom of God around the world. I spread the Word in Nigeria and overseas, where I travel an average of once a month. I have preached the Word in twelve countries including Germany, the United States, Finland, South Africa, Estonia, and Venezuela. Now, I am based in South Africa.

If only my parents had been able to interpret the signs that I was chosen by God! Although my mother had eleven children, I was the only one who moved constantly in her womb, restless to enter the world and become part of God's creation. Because of my family's poverty, I was the only child who was photographed—a lasting image of my early life. Above all, Reverend Dandy, the pastor of my parents' church, had foretold my mother that the

IN THE BEGINNING

child she was bearing had been selected to perform God's work.

My first tangible encounter with God occurred in 1990 and was very dramatic. I had emigrated from the village to live with my elder brother in Iyiowa Odekpe on the outskirts of Onitsha. Poor, illiterate, and lacking any marketable skills, I toiled as a wheelbarrow pusher or porter, ferrying loads for travellers and traders at the Onitsha market. In fact, I worked two jobs. At night, I changed into my Rastafarian clothes and supplemented my meager income by playing my old four-string guitar in nightclubs. As enjoyable as this was, every morning I found myself struggling with the effects of a hangover and sleep deficiency. In order to start work early and make as much money as possible each day, I had to wake up painfully early. I always felt weak to walk the three kilometres to the market. I had no choice because my two jobs began to overlap. As I laboured, I cursed the poverty forced on my family by my father's polygamy.

The night before my encounter with God, I had lived high as usual on booze and marijuana, performing solo at clubs well into the night. On this misty morning as I waded through the fading darkness with ten of my colleagues on our way to the market, I began to pick up signals from the environment. On other days, I almost sleepwalked but not this morning! I could even hear the melody of tenacious birds that had defied the hazards of Onitsha's bustling metropolis. I experienced no hangover, my sight was perfectly clear, and my thoughts were coherent. The reverie of my last performance during the previous evening, where I was given a loud ovation after playing a Bob Marley song, made me happy.

Almost two hundred metres from the market, the clattering sounds of human and vehicular traffic announced that Onitsha was already wide-awake. In response to this reality, we broke into a jog. Suddenly a cool sonorous voice, strong enough to override the noise from the market, cut through the cool morning air.

"Dan, Dan!"

I stopped in my tracks to trace the origin of the call. The voice had certainly not come from any of my colleagues who continued jogging. I looked around quickly, but no one was in sight. I stopped jogging and walked slowly behind my colleagues, but the voice would not leave me. It called me again, only with more urgency this time. The sound of the voice caused goose bumps all over my body. All of a sudden my legs gave way, and I fell face down on the ground. That drew the attention of some of my colleagues. As soon as one of them shouted that it was only epilepsy, they withdrew and left me to my fate.

Moments later, I staggered to my feet, feeling strong again and with my senses restored. As I tried to clean the dirt off my shirt, my friends returned with a volley of questions. The unknown voice also returned, distracting my attention from all the people around me.

"Dan, if you don't repent and serve me, you will die and go to hell. If you don't repent and serve me, you will die and go to hell," the voice echoed in my head, making me clasp my hands over my ears with my head lowered. I was mystified, but the words meant nothing to me. My father had been a pastor but was excommunicated after choosing a second wife. In defiance, he embraced traditional worship and occultism and married two more wives. I grew up ignorant of the ways of God.

I ignored the call and went to work, but the voice would not leave me alone. The message continued to ring in my ears. By noon, I decided to return to Iyiowa Odekpe. With my brother away, I now had the single room to myself. In an attempt to silence the stubborn voice troubling my heart, I smoked marijuana and two cigarettes in quick succession. I wanted to get high and forget the message. However, unlike my previous experiences with marijuana, I felt very normal and still perceptive to the voice. Confused, I dashed to a nearby bar to consume alcohol. Nonetheless, the situation remained the same, and the voice continued to haunt me. Unable to drown the voice out, I had no choice but to accept it.

The day had been difficult for me, but, surprisingly, I

was able to sleep soundly with no interruptions. Yet, the next morning I awoke to the sound of the voice still resonating in my head. It was a Saturday, which was always a busy day for wheelbarrow pushers, but I couldn't go to work. Whenever the voice returned, I had to stop what I was doing. I would clasp my hands desperately over my ears. I was aware that many people believed I was losing my senses. My elder brother attributed the problem to overindulgence in marijuana, and he urged me to stop the habit. He worshipped in front of a small shrine that he kept in one corner of the room we shared. Although I also prayed to my brother's idols, I received no respite from the voice throughout the entire day.

On Sunday morning when the voice awoke me, I found myself in a much-weakened condition. I sat on the bed deciding what to do, until an idea finally came to me. Suspecting that I was not suffering from hallucination but rather that God was in fact calling me, I decided to attend church for the very first time. After a hurried bath, I donned my Rastafarian T-shirt and dirty jeans. I picked up my brother's Bible from the table where it had been gathering dust. A Bible and a shrine in the same small room! I smiled to myself as I wiped the dust off onto my trousers. My brother, who sat quietly watching me the entire time, finally spoke. "Where are you going, young man?"

IN THE BEGINNING

"Church, of course. Where else?"

"So Satan goes to church!" he teased me, roaring with laughter as he rolled on the rickety bed.

I stormed out. Along the way, when the voice rang again in my ears, I returned home for some marijuana. I had decided that if the church service failed to stop the voice, I would finally smoke it out. Upon seeing me again, my brother broke out into another fit of laughter. He never smoked, and he felt my sins were starting to catch up with me.

On that serene Sunday morning, the choice of which neighborhood church to attend became a problem. I shambled past many churches along the way, but when I arrived at a branch of the Grace of God Mission, an inner voice ordered me to enter. At first I resisted. The building was unfinished, and the congregation was too small to represent a good church according to Onitsha standards.

During my moment of indecision, the same inner voice opposed me. "That is the church."

So I thought to myself, *why don't I just pretend I'm going into that church so I can hear what the voice will say next?*

The voice was silent as I made my way into the little church. Upon entering the church, an usher welcomed me and showed me to a seat in the very front row. I felt totally out of place with my dirty clothes, Rastafarian jewellery, and dreadlock hair. I was completely ashamed to be sitting amidst all those people dressed in their Sunday best.

The pastor, a stocky man of fair complexion and dressed like a dandy, was compassionate enough to accept me as I was. He made no comment about my appearance or gave me any curious looks that would have made me feel even more uncomfortable than I already was. He began by preaching the sermon of the day, repeatedly calling on the name of Jesus. Everything he said seemed strange and unfamiliar to me. Soon I drifted into a deep sleep and into a dream of an experience I had nearly seven years earlier.

Seven years before, in Ohaji Egbema, Imo State, I had a terrifying encounter with an evil spirit believed to be the protector of the community's property. After many years of apprenticeship, I had finally qualified as an automobile mechanic, and I was desperate to buy my own tools so I could start work in the city. I joined my father producing palm oil in a mill owned by his friend to earn money to pay for my tools. Despite my efforts, my aspiration remained a dream. Because my father wasn't earning enough money or because he had too many mouths to

IN THE BEGINNING

feed in his large polygamous family, he kept postponing his promise to give me some money.

One night, I made up my mind to sneak into the mill and steal some plastic cans of palm oil. The watchman who happened to be working there was my friend. My father had warned me about an evil spirit that the people called RP for "Rest in Peace." This spirit was believed to protect the property of the villagers, dealing instant death to anyone discovered stealing. However, I rationalised that taking my father's property was not really stealing. I also hoped that RP would lose its power at the mill since the owner was a Jehovah's Witness.

Towards dawn, I was confident that my watchman friend had abandoned his post to drink a local gin called *kaikai*. He was certain to spend the rest of the night with his fat girlfriend. Thus, I snuck into the mill at the outskirts of the village, filling my wheelbarrow with cans of palm oil. As I pushed my load quickly along the deserted road, I noticed a shadowy figure approaching. Knowing that my father often arrived at the mill very early, I assumed the figure was him. I was absolutely terrified that he would skin me alive for stealing. I pushed the wheelbarrow to the edge of the road and slipped into the bush, my breath stifled with fear.

I waited in the bushes, expecting the man to walk past my hiding place, but the all-white human figure, which appeared to have only one leg, didn't appear to be in a hurry. I was very confused. Suddenly, I watched the figure dissolve into a large cloud from which a strong, fierce wind began to blow in my direction.

From the wind came a deep voice announcing, "This is RP."

The voice echoed everywhere, filling me with terror. I can't possibly describe the intense horror I felt. All I remember is feeling as if my body was drying up as the monster approached me. Although the supernatural wind was strong enough to blow down palm trees and my legs felt like jelly, I remained standing.

Suddenly, RP transformed into a human figure that was so massive and tall I couldn't see his face. He walked slowly towards me, shaking the ground violently. As he approached, I felt my body dry up. My throat became parched, my stomach went flat, and I could feel my breath ceasing. When the spirit eventually reached me, I was to him what a Lilliputian was to Gulliver. As he stretched his hand around my waist to lift me up, I felt a dribble of blessed water in my burning stomach. To my relief, I sensed the water flow up into my mouth, creating the sensation that I was about to vomit. However, as soon as I opened my mouth, an involuntary shout of "Jesus" emerged.

At the sound of the name, the wind stopped blow-ing and everything, including RP, stood frozen. At this point, I felt another drop of water in my stomach, which prompted another shout of Jesus. Consequently, the wind seemed to move straight toward a palm tree where it completely dissolved. The palm instantly lurched violently to the right and then to the left. A few moments later, the tree was once again upright, although now withered. At that point, I regained full consciousness and felt human again. Although I knew something inexplicable had happened, the recollection turned hazy later. Everything had been erased from my memory.

I eventually took the oil to the village to sell, but my crime was discovered the following day. The owner of the mill suspected me and reported me to the police for stealing. I was arrested and later sentenced to three years in prison. I started my sentence in an Owerri prison and was later moved to Arochukwu, Ohafia. During my first night at Arochukwu, I had the horrific experience of waking up to discover all the prisoners to my immediate left and right dead. Life in prison was horrible, almost inhuman, and I still count it as one of God's favours that I didn't die there.

Dreaming in the front seat of the church that Sunday, I remembered the encounter with RP for the first time. However, when I shouted "Jesus" as I did in the encounter, I suddenly awoke. I quickly realised that everyone in the church had heard my cry. The pastor replied, "Praise the Lord," to which the startled congregation responded "Hallelujah!" I noticed, as I looked around still bleary from sleep, that I had caused consternation to those good people.

The pastor continued his sermon after my interruption, giving me time to realise my embarrassment. When he finally made the altar call, I was the first person to offer my life to Christ. After the service, I waited to confide in the pastor, who introduced himself as Pastor Oyibo Okechukwu. This kind man turned out to be the good listener I had always desired. At the end of my long story, he advised me that God had saved me because he wanted to use me.

I returned home a very confused man, with the marijuana wraps still in my pocket. The urge to smoke was so strong that I succumbed to my craving and smoked two wraps, but without the high feeling I used to experience before I heard the call. Instead, a feeling of guilt washed over my body.

Heeding the pastor's advice, I decided to review the early indications in my life of God's love for me. I remembered my mother telling me about the prophecy of Reverend Dandy, an American pastor of the Baptist church in our town, after whom I was named. During my mother's pregnancy, he had predicted that the boy she was carry-

PREFACE

ing in her womb would become "a great preacher in this world." So she named me Dan at birth. People thought my name was short for Daniel instead of Dandy.

I also remembered how God saved my life in what I called "the hospital of death." When I was about four years old, I contracted tetanus and was admitted to St. Luke's hospital in Orlu, in Imo State. Thirteen other children suffering from the disease were also admitted to the hospital. Each and every day, one of us died. The implacable course of the disease was so devastating that my father finally confronted the doctor who admitted there were no funds to purchase the required drugs. All the nurses could do was to try to ease the pain and agony of the patients with painkillers.

Within a week, our number had been reduced to five. We all lived with the constant fear of death. Then one afternoon, I noticed a middle-aged man enter the ward to pray for us. After a short prayer, he moved quickly to my bed. He stood quietly for a while, and then told me to pray, "God, I have not done the job you sent me to do, why should I die? God I have not done the job you sent me to do, why should I die?" Soon after the prayer he left.

When my parents visited me later that day, they were surprised to hear me repeating the prayer. "Shut up! Don't say you will die. You're talking rubbish," my mother cried as she broke down in tears.

Astonishingly, when I told them that a preacher had come to pray for us and taught me to say that prayer, my other ward mates denied seeing any such man. Confused, my parents went to confirm my story with the nurses, but they were advised my ward mates were right. I was warned never to talk about death again. When my parents left, I found that prayer was the only thing that gave me relief.

A week later, we were reduced to three in the ward. The doctor advised my father, who was unable to pay the bills, to take me home. Coming home was a nightmare for me. Without the drugs to suppress the pain of my disease, I cried all day, unable to eat or walk. Too poor to buy me drugs, my parents just waited for me to die. My mother maintained silent hope for me, and she continued to pray for my recovery. When I was alone, I repeated the prayer the mysterious preacher had taught me.

One Sunday, as was the practice on Sundays, my mother left me at home to attend the local Anglican Church with my other siblings. The youngest was nine-month-old Ikechukwu Ekechukwu whom we simply called Iyke. My father, who had stopped practising Christianity, hardly ever stayed home on Sundays. So there I was, left alone in the corridor with the door to our rooms locked, to endure my pain and face imminent death. Barely an hour after my family had left for church, I was astonished to see

Iyke. He was walking on his own towards me, where I sat on the floor in pain. I was so shocked I could hardly breathe; I thought I was losing consciousness. When he called out, "Dandy, what are you doing there?" courage surged up within me. His voice was strong and bold just like that of an adult.

"I am sick and disabled and everyone has left me for church," I lamented.

He wouldn't let me finish. "Who said you are crippled? Hold me and stand up," he ordered, offering his hand.

Before I could move, he reached for my hand and lifted me to my feet. He stood there staring at me for a few minutes until he finally let out a triumphant laugh and disappeared.

Suddenly, I felt healthy and strong again. After a quick examination of my body, I noticed that even the sores on my legs had healed. I jumped with joy and started running towards the church.

The church service had ended, and my mother, brothers, and sisters were on their way home when I ran into them.

"What happened?" my mother cried, as I fell into her arms.

When I told her the story, she appeared shocked. "But Iyke never left the church!" Then she fell silent, turning to look at Iyke who was still tied on her back with a piece of cloth. He was asleep. She looked up towards the sky and shouted, "Glory be to God!"

The following day, my father accompanied me to the hospital to confirm I had been healed. The doctor was so shocked that he declined the 200 Naira (about one pound sterling) my father offered him to settle his outstanding bill.

"I didn't heal this boy, God did. And don't forget that all the thirteen other patients in the ward with him have died," the doctor explained.

The recollection of these experiences on the day I first attended church convinced me, without a doubt, of God's love for me. "The pastor is right," I shouted as I jumped about in the room, eager to begin making amends for my questionable past.

I decided to quit smoking marijuana and drinking alcohol, but the withdrawal took such a toll that I found it difficult to eat well. I could only eat one light meal a day. Without food, I was left weak and light-headed. For the first time in my life, I resorted to praying for a solution by combining fasting with prayer. On the third day, I slept before I could break the fast. Around midnight, something strange happened to set me free. In a dream, I saw a huge masquerade leave my body and walk noisily out of our room. Soon after, I awoke feeling very relieved. The following morning, I was strong enough to return to work.

As was my usual practice, I awoke early to rent a wheelbarrow. On the way to my usual location in the market, I heard the voice that had called me the previous week, "Dan, what you are doing is the job of the Egyptians. Drop that wheelbarrow. Remember, you were trained as an automobile mechanic, so return to that trade."

This time I didn't argue with the voice. I returned the wheelbarrow, to the astonishment of my colleagues, and travelled back to my village. My mother was surprised to see my thin appearance.

"What is the problem again?" she asked without even responding to my greeting. "You look so lean, Dan."

"I have a job as a mechanic, so I need my certificate which I gave you to keep." I refused to even sit down while she went to the wooden box where she had kept the document safely.

"I have always believed God will turn things around for you," she stated happily, upon her return. I hugged her and hurried back to the motor park.

Upon arrival in Onitsha later that day, I went straight to the workshop of Elder Boniface, a respected member of the Deeper Life Church, in the Power Line area of Atani Road, where a challenge was awaiting. After accepting my certificate, Elder Boni asked me to demonstrate my skill on a Peugeot car engine that had been dismantled by one of his staff. I uttered a silent prayer and went to work. Approximately an hour later, I started the engine with a roar and received applause from all the workers. That same day, I was employed on an allowance of 600 Naira per month.

That was considered a lot of money back then. I saved as much as I could and used it to open my own workshop. However, I ensured the growth of my spiritual life as well. At church, I had become a worker and leader of the evangelism team. I prayed day and night and had become a humble and respectable man, but to my surprise, my brother, who still kept the deity in our room, told me the room was too small to accommodate both of us. With the help of our pastor, I moved in with another church member until I could rent a room for myself almost three months later. Meanwhile, I continued my spiritual growth.

two

In Ministry

From that point on, my interest in the works of God intensified so much that I could hardly do anything but work in the service of God. Armed with a rustic bell, I found myself rising with the dawn, preaching, and proclaiming the Good News of the Gospel in the streets of Iyiowa Odekpe.

My initial fascination with my occupation as an automobile mechanic gradually declined. At work, I took advantage of every possible opportunity to evangelize my colleagues. Although they poked fun at me, I was not the least perturbed. My sole concern was how to increase my dawn audience. I had heard somebody complain about not understanding Igbo language and not being able to receive the message of salvation I was proclaiming. Undeterred, I continued and even committed my inadequacy in

English to the Lord. He is, and has always been, a strong tower when you call on him. As a testimony, I started preaching in English the following day. Today I am able to deliver the message of the Lord positively anywhere. As a dropout at primary three level without any formal training, this remains an astonishing achievement.

Led by the Holy Spirit, I officially began full-time ministry in January 1994. One morning, the voice of God ordered me to visit Oraifite, a town where I knew no one. I only passed through the town whenever I had to go to my village, Amaimo, several kilometresfrom the Imo State capital of Owerri. I hesitated, completely bewildered. However, in obedience to the Lord, I packed my bag, headed to the motor park and boarded a minibus en route to Oraifite. On the way, I was excited to contemplate what lay ahead of me. This was my first missionary journey, and I was already visualizing great challenges. Upon arrival in Oraifite, my fear heightened; I didn't know where to exit the bus or how to begin. As the bus conductor called out for the passengers who would exit at the Nkwo Oraifite, the Oraifite market, I decided to alight there. This would give me a feel of the town where God had sent me.

It was there that my first test in the service of God began. I left the bus, trying to get my bearings. Moments later, a mad woman, whose popular name I later discovered to be Nwafurutu, jumped at me in a belligerent manner. She started shouting at me, questioning why I had come to Oraifite. I was moved by the Holy Spirit to pray for her. Eventually, I managed to calm the poor woman; whereupon, she fell into a deep sleep.

A crowd had gathered to watch the encounter and to witness how the power of God was manifested in the way I subdued the mad woman. A man stepped out and inquired if I was a pastor. As I was not a pastor when I made that particular journey, I couldn't answer in the affirmative. I was only a child of God and a preacher of the Gospel of Jesus Christ. I told him that I wasn't a pastor and introduced myself as a servant of God. He introduced himself as Emma Oguego, an elder in the Grace of God Mission, Oraifite. To my amazement, he offered me accommodation, which became the base where I started evangelism.

Soon, the Holy Spirit inspired me to start holding prayer meetings at Oguego's residence. As the congregation grew, we requested to use the Town Hall, which was granted. Months later, some people who felt threatened, rose against the use of the Town Hall. Almost immediately, an appreciative family donated a parcel of land to us. With the grace of the Holy Spirit, I was able to release many people in the town who worshipped idols from spiritual bondage. That accomplishment put my life in danger. However, Almighty God, who led me to Oraifite, faithfully abided with me.

In one of the many instances, the Ibenwa family appealed to me to destroy a shrine that had kept every family that had served it, including theirs, in poverty and death. The family complained that they were tired of serving the idol. They explained that they had called the villagers repeatedly to remove the idol but to no avail. My investigation revealed that the villagers were afraid. They were aware that individuals who took custody of the idol were ensnared by suffering and invited death into their family. Therefore, when the Ibenwa family appealed to me in desperation, I had no choice but to deliver them from spiritual bondage.

We planned to destroy the idol. At midnight on the agreed date, I led my prayer warriors to the location where I tore down the shrine, destroyed the idol, burned all the paraphernalia, and then conducted a deliverance service for the family.

The work of God in Oraifite endeared me to many families such as the Umeze family, who donated the piece of land to us. It was to show appreciation for delivering Ekene, a member of the family, who had a fetish and wore masks during festivals.

Another incident in the course of my walk with God in Oraifite is worth recounting. In this town, as in most Igbo towns and communities, pythons are highly regarded as sacred reptiles. In most cases, these creatures are venerated. Consequently, no one ever harmed a python. However, on one occasion, a python threatened to attack me. I defended myself by killing it. This drew the ire of the entire community. Nonetheless, the Lord God bestowed upon me the spirit of boldness to confront the challenges as they rapidly unfolded.

My evangelism experience in Oraifite was as demanding as it was interesting. I met the lady who is currently my wife in Oraifite. We met in 1994 while she was still a Banking and Finance student at Madonna University, Okija, near Oraifite. I proposed to her late in 1995, but her parents would hear nothing of it. Her father, in particular, was vehemently opposed to the idea of his daughter marrying me because I was poor.

One day, I even overheard them scolding her angrily, "We sent you to the university to obtain a degree, and all you could do is pay us back with this dirty pastor as a suitor."

Completely convinced that the two of us were incompatible, they did everything possible to frustrate me. They reminded her innumerable times that they were doing me a favour by accommodating me in their house because I was working for God. Their opposition continued until late 1996, but it never diminished my love for Nneka.

Eventually her family relented. We held the traditional wedding on December 31, 1996, and were joined in holy wedlock on February 9, 1997.

My ministry generated considerable furor in Oraifite and caused much frustration in the build-up to my marriage. For instance, some of my in-laws discredited me to the community by reporting that I had killed a python and destroyed a shrine. Killing a python was an abomination and Nneka's father, being a traditionalist, branded me an enemy of the Igbo tradition. I was "guilty" of those two acts. However, I was convinced that they would not have generated that much tension if not for my landlord and prospective father-in-law. He had incensed the people of Oraifite to drive me out of the Town Hall in an effort to stop me from marrying his daughter! The village was now sufficiently roused to fight me, and they went as far as to kidnap and attempt to murder me.

At the peak of the crisis, some of the elders of the community summoned me to explain what they referred to as "my mischief." At the venue, I refused to perform the traditional lining of the face with local chalk. I also refused to imitate them by drawing weird lines around my seat before sitting. I just walked in, took a seat, and waited for the elders to arrive. When they had completed their rituals, they announced my offences: I had killed a python and destroyed a traditional shrine of worship. They said my offences were indisputable because my father-in-law himself had compiled it.

According to their tradition, the community would bury a python that had been killed with all the rituals of a human funeral. Consequently, they ordered me to provide a befitting burial to the snake or else leave town within seven days. I never denied the accusations, but walked up to their leader and asked him, "Chief, why are you saying this? You know that so many people have sat on the seat that you are occupying now. Where are those people now? That seat belongs to God. Anyone who is in it must be held accountable for whatever he does to none other than God."

My effrontery obviously shocked him. "Chief," I continued, "God sent me to this village. If God tells me I should go, I will go. But God has not yet told me I should leave."

Then I turned to the rest of the elders to explain that I killed the python in self-defense after it tried to attack me. They covered their ears with their hands and shouted with palpable rage, "Abomination!"

They claimed the python was a gentle snake that never hurt anybody. I fearlessly disagreed and insisted that the reptile had in fact threatened me.

Then they demanded an explanation for the destruction of the shrine. The shrine had been destroyed at midnight, and only the Ibenwa family, who were custodians of the shrine, knew that I had done it with the assistance of my prayer warriors. I knew they never told anyone about the incident. However, the rumour mill had been activated and accusing fingers all pointed at me. I knew that the elders were only trying to confirm the rumour, so I didn't deny destroying the shrine. I explained that I had done so not only at the behest of the Ibenwa family, who wished to be liberated from the shackles of the shrine, but also the villagers who made it abundantly clear how tired they had grown of the shrine. Unfortunately, my explanation didn't satisfy them.

Their decision was quick and simple: Leave the town! The judgment didn't disconcert me. Again, I rose to my feet and addressed them. I told them I wouldn't leave because God had sent me. I watched them gnash their teeth in suppressed rage. I was determined to stay. I told them they were wrong. An uneasy silence fell over the venue.

I seized the opportunity to further reinforce my point: "When I entered here, I greeted everybody respectfully. All the others who arrived later did the same to those who were seated in similar fashion."

Then I turned to their leader, and told him, "I know you are a member of the Anglican Church. When I entered this hall, someone greater than all of us came in with me.

That person was the Lord Jesus." I expected everyone to hallow him; although, no one did. My comments drew a heavy silence over the chambers.

Seconds later, some of the chiefs began to shout, calling me a stupid, irreverent boy. Some of them furiously reiterated their judgment that I should leave town in less than a week. Some of the traditional medicine men proceeded to pronounce a curse, which I knew, would have no effect on me as a child of God. While all this was happening, their leader remained completely calm and never uttered a single word.

Suspecting that he was considering my case, I insisted that he judge fairly. This way, he would avoid the judgment of God who had the almighty power to remove him and replace him with someone else, if he judged wrongly. By then, I had exhausted the limit of their tolerance. The elders yelled and stamped their feet and caused near pandemonium. They accused me of placing a curse on their leader. Rushing toward me, they lifted me up with a fury that belied their age and status in the community.

Their leader broke his lengthy silence for the first time and ordered them to put me down. They complied immediately. He asked me to leave the venue forthwith but insisted that I leave within one week. I left the venue but not the town. Meanwhile, some of the men had their own plan for me. The traditional medicine men, who accused me of ruining their business, were bent on destroying or killing me. People who suffered spiritual problems and ailments were leaving the medicine men in droves to attend my church, where God was doing wonders.

One of those heady nights, six of the medicine men, dressed in traditional war regalia with charms dangling from their necks, stormed into my house and ordered me out. They led me along a bush path to a nearby stream. With the stream in sight, they stopped, chanted some incantations, stripped me naked, and ordered me to walk to the stream alone. Shivering with fear, the implication was crystal clear to me—they would shoot me as soon as I stepped into the stream.

With locally made guns pointed at me, I had no choice. I couldn't turn to fight them, but I could pray. I prayed as I approached the stream. When I arrived at the banks, my Saviour showed His might yet again.

"Dan, you are more powerful than those people. They can't kill you; they can't kill you," thundered the familiar voice that had called me to service. I stopped in my tracks. As I covered my face with my palms to thank God, I felt currents of courage surging within me. I turned promptly and marched to where the medicine men stood chanting incantations. When I got there, all the men appeared to have fallen into a deep sleep. I stood there staring at them in amazement of God's power. I successfully resisted the temptation to kill them and returned home. Today, thanks to the glory of God, one of the men is a priest of the Anglican Church in Oraifite.

Almost three weeks after the encounter with the elders, the community began to experience a shakeup. The leader of the elders went to meet his ancestors, and an elder who had summoned the police to arrest me falsely so I would leave town, hanged himself. The man I hardly knew had lodged a complaint against me with the police. After the police interrogated me, they discovered that the man had lied, so I was never arrested.

This incident took place on a Friday. On Monday, I heard that the man had mysteriously hanged himself behind his own house. This last death compounded the challenges faced by my ministry in Oraifite. The villagers vainly accused me of murder.

This new twist was accompanied by a further manifestation of the awesome power of God.

At one of our night vigils, we noticed an unusual presence in the congregation of worshippers. Unknown to us, she was an emissary of one of the most dreaded traditional medicine men in a neighbouring town. During the vigorous praise worship, the power of God came down forcefully. This emissary, whose name we later discovered to be Ngozi, was visited by the might of the Holy Spirit.

The fire of God felled her, and she screamed and rolled

on the floor in full view of the entire congregation. As the prayers reached a crescendo, the miraculous happened! To everyone's astonishment, she vomited one razor blade and eleven office pins before slumping over into a deep sleep. She remained asleep even at the end of the vigil when the congregation had dispersed. The prayer warriors later brought her to my house to pray earnestly for her soul.

During prayer, we discovered that she was the daughter of a well-known traditional medicine man. We continued praying for her until approximately 11:30 a.m. when her father arrived at my residence.

I greeted him, but he simply asked, "Are you Pastor Dan?"

I answered yes.

At which point, he stated, "The power that did this is not a small power." He turned around and walked out.

Some of my people thought he had left to summon the police, but we weren't afraid, thanks to our full trust in God. We continued to pray and thank God, hopeful that more revelations would come from Ngozi. The Police arrived later, but they were satisfied with our explanation of Ngozi's current condition.

By the grace of God, she recovered in the evening and gave us enlightening testimonies. She told us that her father often sent her to perform ritual attacks. Although thirty office pins and one razor blade had been implanted in her, she had vomited only the razor blade and eleven of the pins. She claimed to transform herself regularly into a python to patrol the track roads, especially the road leading to the riverside. Since pythons were held sacred in Oraifite, anybody who encountered her in her transformed state wouldn't harm her. However, she would attack and bite anyone who walked alone, because no one could testify that a python was the attacker in such a situation. She would transmit one office pin into her victim's body, which ensured that no one would ever be able to reveal what had bitten him or her. She claimed the razor blade also gave her the power to abort women's pregnancies.

The powerful manifestation of God's supremacy promoted my work, and the Ministry grew beyond Oraifite. As more people identified and worshipped with us, we were able to build a befitting worship centre on the land donated by the Umeze family.

God's seizure of Ngozi and her subsequent revelations did little to change the minds of the people who were still hell-bent on my expulsion from Oraifite. When some of the people who had confronted me began to die one after the other, I became a prime suspect. Amidst the tense atmosphere, my prospective father-in-law passed on.

One night, I received an unusual visitor—a mad woman who knocked on my door. This was the second time I was accosted by a mad woman in Oraifite. She was well-known in the community and had an exclusive spot she always occupied in the community square. When I opened the door, she confronted me immediately. "You are still here. Don't you know that you will die today?"

That angered me. "I bind you in the name of Jesus," I retorted.

She ran away at lightning speed, and I immediately began to pray, pleading the blood of Jesus. Then the voice returned with its unambiguous message: "Leave now." In obedience, I gathered a few of my belongings, vacated the house, and returned to Onitsha. Unbeknownst to me, that was the same day my father-in-law's corpse was brought home for the commencement of the funeral rites. I didn't know about this because I had moved out of there over the problems arising from my intention to marry Nneka. Her father's death made everybody so angry with Nneka that she too was forced to flee her home. Her flight severed any contact I had with the family; although, I knew they wanted my life as well.

During the funeral wake-keeping programme that evening, some young boys carried the corpse on their heads and searched for me around town in Oraifite. When they arrived at the house I had vacated, they forced open the door to my room, but I wasn't there. Led by the dreaded *Ayaka* masquerade, they left to search for me at the church, still carrying the corpse and singing. In a fit of frustration and rage, they set the church ablaze, destroying everything inside. In Igbo culture, the masquerade represents the spirit and human worlds. It is generally believed in the Igboland that the masquerade is a spirit that springs from the soil. Each masquerade possesses particular attributes (warrior-like prowess, mystical powers, youthfulness, and old age) and specializes in one or more skills (dancing skills, acrobatics, and other ritual manifestations). The masquerade appears during traditional celebrations (funerals) and festivals (new yam festival). The *Ayaka* masquerade was dreaded, for what the traditional worshippers believe it to be is strong mystical powers and the militancy of some of its adherents.

After the devastation, they encircled the church area with palm fronds to indicate that it was now an abandoned property that belonged to the community deity. According to their tradition, the ownership of any place that the *Ayaka* masquerade destroys reverts to the deity.

On my return to Oraifite days later, I headed straight to the church premises. I was agonized by the sight of the wreckage. Furiously, I removed the objects the masquerade and the community had used to encircle my church. I wandered through the black ashes, looking for anything to salvage. As I continued searching amidst the destruction, I foresaw the hardships I would undergo to rebuild the church; tears welled in my eyes.

Everything burned and destroyed! However, I continued rummaging the wreckage. Suddenly, I noticed something in the rubble that testified to the greatness of God. At the spot where the altar stood I saw part of the spine of my Bible. The piece was covered in ashes, and I assumed the rest of the Bible must have been burned with the other church property. As I bent over to pick it up, I was immediately relieved to note its unscathed condition.

I screamed, "My Bible didn't burn!" I held it to my chest, like the lamb that was once lost but later found. This had been my first Bible. I bought it from a member of the Deeper Life Bible Church at the mechanic workshop during the time I offered my life to Jesus Christ. This was the beautiful Bible that I used in my formative years in the Christian ministry. I still have it today because I consider it a special treasure.

From the wreckage, I went to the house where I had been living. I discovered that my room had also been ransacked; although, nothing had been taken. The robbers must have been very surprised to discover nothing more than a foam mattress on the bare floor and a few plastic chairs! My co-tenants advised me that they had to hang the door on the doorframe to safeguard my few possessions from prying eyes.

Once again, I reviewed the whole incident, and I was scared the attackers might have gone to the Umeze compound, where a room was reserved for the musical instruments, to complete their havoc! Thank God that a member of the church named Eme had taken safe custody of the instruments.

Given all the destruction and the rumours of further action from my attackers, I realized it would be prudent to retreat from the town. Therefore, I left for Onitsha, wondering how I would start all over again. While meditating on the best way to move forward, I recalled one manager at the Delta Steel Company in Warri who had been very close to our ministry.

His identification with us started when I first ministered to him and his wife. The opportunity arose through the Full Gospel Business Men Fellowship in Onitsha. I prayed for them, and the Lord answered those prayers when the woman became pregnant. During the difficult delivery, the man had sent for me to pray for his wife. A few moments after the prayer, the baby arrived, and they named him after me. My association with the family grew stronger after the baby's birth. From then on they welcomed me with open arms. They never withheld any support. They offered me money without me asking, and they were about to help me pay for better accommodation at Oraifite after my last debacle.

Consequently, when I left Oraifite, I headed straight to visit them in Warri. I narrated my plight, and they hosted me in their official flat promising to help me secure accommodation in the company's residential area. The man advised me we would need to raise almost twenty thousand naira to pay for the accommodation once it was allocated. After a few days, I returned to Onitsha in search of money.

While I was searching for money, thoughts of Ifeoma resurfaced. Ifeoma was a lady I had met during the challenges to my work with God at Oraifite.

Nneka and I had completely lost contact since the passing of her father. Her family's anger had forced her to run away from home while precipitating my own expulsion from the community. It was in this state of torment that I met Ifeoma. By modest standards, she was not a penurious lady. Although she was a native of Oraifite, she lived and worked in Lagos. She knew of my relationship with Nneka and the many troubles we encountered. She showed such a great interest in me and showered me with so much money and gifts that I began to develop an interest in her. However, in my heart, I knew I didn't love her. I suspected that her interest in me arose more out of sympathy for what I had to endure.

The effort of raising money for the Delta Steel accommodation rent led me to her place in Lagos. I didn't know exactly where she lived. However, I remembered her telling me she worshipped at the Bethel Assembly, and I still had that address. I chose a Sunday morning to meet her at church to verify whether she would still honour her promises of support. I arrived in Lagos on an overnight bus service. With no time to bathe, I located the church, participated in the service, and met her afterwards. We went to her home where I discussed the deterioration of the situation at Oraifite and my decision to settle elsewhere.

Not only did she give me more than the twenty thousand Naira needed for the accommodation in Warri, she also showered me with gifts. She suggested delicately that I spend the night. I declined the offer, telling her I couldn't sleep in Lagos as I had to return to Onitsha that same day.

With the money firmly in hand, I returned to the family in Warri to start the process of securing the promised accommodation. I spent three weeks in their house praying for my dream of starting afresh to materialise.

By the time it got to my turn on the day the apartments were allocated, the man in charge, called Joseph, told me there were no more houses available. I was the last person and the only one left. My host returned home, his face a picture of fury and disappointment. He consoled me by reassuring me he would persuade them to rescind the decision the following day, but his attempt was unsuccessful. The next day, they refunded my twenty thousand naira. I interpreted the experience as a sign that God didn't want me to live in Warri.

I took the money, retraced my steps, and returned to Onitsha to resuscitate my ministry. I immediately paid for locally assembled instruments and promised to pick them up later.

Afterwards, I headed to Oraifite to check on the state of the church equipment we had left in the care of the Umeze family. I needed them as a backup. At Oraifite, the man refused to surrender anything to me unless all the members of the congregation were reassembled. I failed to discover his subterfuge until his sister, a member of the Deeper Life Ministry, pulled me aside and explained that her brother had sold all the equipment to a man in Obosi, near Onitsa, called Mojo.

Armed with the details provided by the lady, I traced the receiver of the musical items to Obosi. When I asked a commercial motorcyclist to lead me to Mojo's residence, he stared at me with bewilderment and wondered aloud why I wanted to go there! Noticing his reticence, I introduced myself and explained that I had a commission to go and preach to Mojo. People had warned me to be careful with him stating, "The man is evil."

I later hired a stocky, brave motorbike operator, but the best he could do was to stop metres away from Mojo's dreaded residence. When he pointed the way, intense fear gripped me. I uttered a silent prayer, and as I got there I summoned my courage and knocked at the gate.

Three hefty, fearsome boys showed up at the gate and demanded to know who I was and what I wanted. With surging boldness, I asked to see their boss, Mojo. They sneered at me, invited me into the living room, and ordered me to take a seat by the staircase. One of them watched over me while the other two left. My "guard" never said a word to me as the atmosphere assumed a foreboding air. After what seemed like an eternity, the sound of heavy measured footsteps descending the stairs signalled an encounter that would remain forever ingrained in my memory. As I turned to see who was coming down the stairs, my eyes locked on the corrosive and intimidating eyes of a colossus. His enormous stature was even more pronounced by his near nakedness; he wore only underpants. He dramatized his descent to the living room, exuding the swagger of a lion set to devour its victim. He stopped midway and asked in a deadly voice, "Who is the person looking for Mojo?"

I was so overcome with fear that I couldn't tell him the reason for my visit. I simply told him I was a pastor and that I had come to preach the Gospel of Jesus Christ.

His eyes suddenly turned red as he ordered, "Gospel? Take your Bible and get out of this place. If I ever see you here again, I will eat you raw."

I got up and made a hasty retreat to the door. At the gate, it suddenly occurred to me that I had not prayed. Right there and then, I said a short prayer. As I prayed, the unmistakable voice ordered me, "Go back!"

I returned and knocked at the door again. Just like the first time, I waited until his boys appeared to walk me out.

I refused to give up. I resorted to screaming at the top of my lungs that it wasn't proper for him to treat a man of God this way and that I had come from Oraifite for my Church musical equipment, which had been sold to him. While I was shouting, Mojo came down, still in his underpants and breathing fire. By that time, I was standing by his gate. As he approached, I was led by the Spirit of God to say, "If you don't bring the equipment within one week, you must beg for bread to eat." I then turned and left. The people at the scene were very surprised that I would challenge such a man.

When I left, I had no idea what else to do. The family whose room I had rented before the *Ayaka* masquerade destruction had repossessed their accommodation. So I decided to shuttle between Onitsha and Oraifite. I did this for some time until the Ibenwa family accommodated me through their son, Rapuruchukwu, who was an unemployed graduate. He offered me his room as a born-again Christian and a member of our ministry. It was a known fact that since I was declared a *persona non grata*, anybody who dared to host me risked the ire of the entire community. This decision also meant that the family would receive an unusual visitation from the *Ayaka*, the dreaded masquerade—who, according to tradition, did not venture out during the day.

Consequently, I was using that room secretly in order to avoid suspicion. The man who sold my equipment was close to the Ibenwa family, and he knew that I lived in the family home. That was why exactly one week after the Obosi encounter with Mojo, Ekene led the dreaded man to me. One evening, I was reading my Bible under an orange tree when they appeared.

Mojo was the first one to speak. He recounted how he had been desperately looking for me. He said he had been experiencing all sorts of trouble since our first encounter. His cars were seized because the company he had entered into a deal with had failed. He wanted to know if I meant the pronouncement that I had made earlier.

I confirmed that I wasn't joking about him returning the equipment that belonged to my pastoral ministry to avoid the wrath of the Almighty God. The next morning, he arrived with one of his friends to pick me up. Initially, I expressed some reservation, but the spirit of God advised me to go with them. I decided to comply.

The first place we arrived at was the studio of a radio mechanic. He ordered the man to fetch the amplifier immediately because it belonged to the church. The man wasted no time bringing out the amplifier. Next, we visited a disk jockey who quickly handed over the loudspeakers. In each case, he threatened to report in the case to the police if they refused to surrender the musical equipment they had bought from him. Lastly, we arrived at his house where we picked up the wireless microphone and the rest of the equipment that he had not yet sold. He delivered them to my Ibenwa family abode the same day. I prayed for him and sent him off with a promise that I would see him the following day.

When I arrived at his house the next day, he confirmed many of the rumours I had heard from gossips. He acknowledged that he was the leader of a very strong confraternity in Obosi and that his wife was the leader of the women's group. He also explained the level he had attained within the hierarchy of the confraternity and many other things he had done. I preached salvation to him; I told him that Jesus Christ is the only way and the authority above all authorities. I asked him to submit to the salvation and authority of Christ. I left him and continued shuttling between Onitsha and Oraifite with the occasional visit to him. Six months had passed, and even though I had recovered all of my equipment, I still hadn't settled down in any particular place to start my ministry. However, this didn't stop me from going to pray with him.

One day, while I was preaching to him, I overheard his wife complain that there was no food at home. I couldn't believe the situation was that bleak! I was moved to give him some money to tide him over temporarily. That action appeared to be the motivation he needed because his eyes seemed to suddenly open to my preaching. He developed a greater interest and confessed more often.

Based on the stories he told me, I knew the confraternity held him in bondage. The only way out, I advised him, was the destruction of the confraternity's paraphernalia. I kept encouraging him to free his mind of the fear that he would be killed if he renounced his membership and position in the group.

Finally, both husband and wife repented and accepted Jesus Christ as their Lord and Saviour. The man led me to a room where all the voodoo objects were safely guarded. We brought all of them out and burnt everything to ashes. After that, they kept explaining how their former colleagues regularly haunted them. Undaunted, I continued to pray with and for them. I encouraged them not to waiver but rather to hold on solidly to Jesus Christ as their Lord and Master. I also told him one last thing we needed to do in order to stop them from harassing him was for him to declare in an open assembly that he had repented and given his life to Jesus Christ. Many prayers and a long time later, he was finally persuaded to make such an open confession.

Coincidentally, that open confession by Mojo also marked the rebirth of my ministry. Many fervent prayers and careful planning was required. I had to convince Mojo to provide a photograph of himself in his confraternity regalia depicting his level. The photograph was used in a poster that was widely circulated to invite the entire Obosi community to the crusade. We also had a banner which screamed, "Mojo of Obosi now a child of God: Come and hear him expose the confraternity mysteries." Getting him to accept was a Herculean task, but God was with us. The posters attracted the attention of people who were eager to watch him.

IN MINISTRY

By this time, Nneka and I had gotten back together. Neither the desires of the flesh nor the glitters of the world could put asunder what God had ordained. Not even the afflictions of man! When I returned to Oraifite, I found her, but I was beholden to Ifeoma because of the gifts she had bestowed upon me. I knew that Nneka was my ordained wife. However, I was still appreciative of the role Ifeoma played in resettling me. Although she wanted us to marry, I kept our relationship a platonic one. When the two ladies met in my house one day, I knew the time to confirm my choice had finally arrived. Both Nneka and I remained quiet while Ifeoma began ranting for Nneka to leave me alone. All through the encounter, Nneka remained calm. In the end, Ifeoma demanded that I return all the gifts she had given me: the suits, ties, and shoes. I returned all of them immediately with a promise to refund her twenty thousand naira at a later date. After I repaid the debt, the Ifeoma chapter ended.

Nneka became part of the congregation at the Obosi Town Hall, even though we were still not married. That first day of the crusade was great. Every single space in the hall was occupied with many more people perching on any available platform outside. That was the first time I had ever preached before such a large crowd. They didn't come to hear me preach. In fact, they didn't know anything about me. They came to hear Mojo speak in the congregation of God's faithful—the dreaded Mojo who was linked to the kidnapping of children in Obosi; Mojo the terror who would break down people's houses unchallenged; Mojo the "strong man" who, because he donated the land on which the police station was built, was considered to be a friend of the police. Everybody wanted to hear him speak. When I took the microphone, I was moved in spirit to sing a song, and I encouraged the entire congregation to join me.

During the singing, the spirit of God ministered to me that an agent of darkness was waiting in the congregation to harm me. I announced the revelation immediately and requested that he either come forward and be saved or face the consequences. Nobody moved and the entire hall was silent. I repeated the statement, with no success, but I was undaunted. At that point, I continued with the worship songs. I unconsciously started singing the "Jehovah Jireh" song and the congregation joined in immediately. As the singing gained momentum, a young, handsome man was hauled up and thrown to the floor! He rolled and screamed "fire, fire," immediately attracting everyone's attention. The crowd watched him in amazement until he stood up, placed his hands in his pocket and brought out a charm.

He confessed that he had been sent by Mojo's confraternity as an agent of marine spirits. He explained that two men had come, but the other man had left as soon as I made the pronouncement. He had chosen to stay back because he believed he could still attack me and disrupt the crusade. Now limp, he lay there at the altar until the end of the crusade.

God's arrest of this young man didn't diminish the crowd's expectations for Mojo's testimony. Because I had planned for it to last three nights of the crusade, the testimony that first night was brief. Afterwards, I preached and prayed. After the crusade, we took the young man to Mojo's residence where he was given a place to sleep. The next morning when we awoke, the young man was gone. Nobody knew how he had left. The doors and the gate to the house were still firmly locked, but the man was nowhere to be found.

The remaining two days of the crusade were also eventful. Mojo concluded his testimonies with shocking many revelations. He explained the process of his initiation into the confraternity and how he rose to be their leader. He also described his encounter with God, which eventually led to the open renouncement of his membership at the crusade. The testimony and the crusade really helped to kick-start my ministry in Obosi.

On the last day of the crusade, I announced that we would commence weekly fellowships at that same venue every Monday evening. The programme subsequently began with Mojo and his wife actively participating. The fellowship grew very rapidly. People came from near and far, bringing the sick and the afflicted with them to the packed hall. While I was in Obosi, God gave me a special mission: to heal mad people. To His Glory, many of these people were healed. So the Holy Spirit urged me to continue. Because of God's wonderful work, people kept bringing more people for healing. As their population grew, I had to quarter them at the boys' section of a flat that I had received from a woman I saved from constant spiritual attack.

The healing of mad people presented its own challenges; once in a while, they would break loose, but Nneka would run after them, round them up, and place chains on them. She accomplished this task very effectively with the assistance of the guard who manned the security gate. However, she found the situation in the compound too busy, noisy, and unacceptable, and so she asked me to leave. I even tried to host some of the individuals in my flat, but it was still difficult to contain them. Eventually Nneka and I decided to abandon housing them. Instead, we would pray for them whenever they were led in by their people. They would then be taken home right after prayers.

My ministry experienced significant growth at Obosi, and we were able to gradually regain facilities for effective evangelization. I had started out humbly with a serviceable Peugeot station wagon that I had purchased from Nneka's family because nobody else would buy it. With the ministry's name boldly written on it, the vehicle was used strictly for evangelism, particularly for carrying the church equipment to various venues. However, it broke down almost daily. A family eventually donated a Mercedes Benz 230 as a way of offering thanks to God for answering their prayers. Their son had suffered a lingering problem for three years, and his father had approached me to intercede with God for deliverance from that problem.

The God of infinite mercy, whose sun shines compassionately on everyone, answered our prayers. The offering of the Mercedes Benz was a pleasant surprise.

From Obosi, I moved the ministry to a nearby town called Nkpor, which was much larger than Obosi. In the course of evangelism to the nearby community of Allor, an only son of a family came to me with a gory story. He had five sisters, but his father was not content with just one son.

The father married another wife. However, in his old age, people speculated that he could not have been the father of the woman's two sons. Unfortunately, the woman contracted a strange illness, which source the people couldn't trace. At the terminal stage, she left her matrimonial home for her father's home, alleging that she had been poisoned. She died there, but the corpse was returned for burial in her husband's compound in Allor.

The Allor villagers accepted the corpse and buried her, but they remained mindful of the accusations. After the burial, problems poured down in quick succession: the children of the first wife began to experience mental disorders starting with the first daughter. The second daughter suffered the same fate almost immediately afterwards. The problem spread to the only son in a distant Asian country where he had gone on a business trip. While he was there, a tortoise from their village idol that his father used to worship appeared to him in a dream. That tortoise was known to have killed rich men in their community. The community believed that anybody who saw the tortoise in a dream would surely die. In the dream, the tortoise pulled at his leg. By this time, his elder sisters had already been sent to a psychiatric hospital, while one lived in an Owerri prayer house.

When he came to me, I asked him to lead me to the land where the deity was located. He expressed fear, claiming that snakes and tortoises were known to emerge from that area to attack people. I calmed his fears and insisted we travel there. We prayed and went there together. I studied the small strange bush for a while and then left.

On the appointed day for me to destroy the deity, he arrived from Lagos. Together with my prayer warriors, we went to the shrine housing the moulded deity and broke it down. Underneath, the idol was soft as dust. When we removed the dust, a large snake sprang out at us. Everybody ran, but I stood my ground and focused on the reptile. Suddenly, the Holy Spirit instructed me to touch the creature. I stretched out my hand, and the snake recoiled. Then, I reached out for a stick to kill it but was surprised to discover it had already died.

We then gathered some firewood to set fire to it, but the man suddenly changed his mind. He became annoyed and flatly refused to let us burn the snake! He said I could take the creature elsewhere to burn but not there. I placed the snake into the trunk of my car and headed straight to my compound of eight flats. I placed the snake under the staircase, climbed upstairs to my second floor flat, and told my wife, Nneka, the whole story.

That night, everyone in the compound was spiritually attacked, and they were all praying so loudly, Nneka joined them. While everybody was shouting Holy Ghost Fire, the spirit of God told me that the idol I brought to the premises in the name of the dead snake was the cause of the attacks. I joined in the prayer, and calm returned. People went to sleep.

The next morning, the young man came to my house to enquire what I had done with the snake. I refused to tell him how the snake idol had disturbed the sleep of my co-tenants all night. So we both took the snake out to burn it thoroughly in a lonely place. When I emptied the sack in which I had kept it, I noticed that the dead snake had turned into a live tortoise! That didn't frighten me for I knew that the end had come for the demon. We killed the tortoise. To ensure that it was actually dead, we soaked it with car fuel, ignited it, and saw it burn completely. Since then, the young man has remained a source of great financial assistance to the ministry.

The destruction of the deity saved him from mental disorientation. He later came to narrate his sisters' illnesses. On my advice, he brought them. As I looked at them, the Holy Spirit told me that the source of the problem with his sisters was in their house. I advised him that we would need to pray with them in the family compound.

On the agreed date, I visited their well-fortified compound. While we were praying, I was led in spirit to a grave in the compound. At that time, I had never heard the story about their stepmother. The grave was encircled by three chains with another one used as a design on short iron poles that held the chains together. The spirit of God explained to me that the chains had been used to hold down the spirit of the sisters' stepmother.

After the prayer, the Spirit of God told me that we should dig up the grave to remove the charms that were buried within. I told the man what we should do.

"Abomination! How can we go and dig up a grave!" the man resisted.

He was afraid to be called a ritualist. I suggested that he invite the villagers to witness the exercise. Finally, we had to honour his decision and return his sisters to the psychiatric hospital. However, one month later, he suffered a very severe headache, the type that his sisters experienced previously. Convinced the grave might be the cause of the problem, he invited me to carry out the exercise. Some of the villagers and members of the family were present at the event, and his sisters had been brought back home.

As usual, I went with my prayer warriors. The village boys demanded fifty thousand naira to dig up the grave. They claimed digging up a grave was considered an abomination in their culture if certain rites weren't performed. Some Hausa labourers were hired to do the job for much less. In fact, they never knew it was a grave. It wasn't until they arrived at the coffin that they realised what was happening. The situation stung them like a bee—an abomination had been committed! They immediately surrendered, laid down their digging implements and left in a huff. The man ran after them and paid them their money. They had already done enough.

Together with the prayer warriors, we used shovels to clear the sand before removing the coffin, which still looked fresh even after six years. The coffin contained a neatly arranged skeleton. The hair was still visible on the skull. Guided by the Holy Spirit of God, I shifted the head and was baffled by what I saw. Six charms were tied in a knot, and two of them had broken open as if they were set on fire, while the remaining four remained intact.

The genesis of the family's problem had been unearthed. Everybody marvelled and praised God. We burned the coffin and its contents and sealed the grave. I prayed and anointed the entire compound. During the prayer, God's glory was being manifested. The sisters started regaining sanity, and they began to talk coherently as they joined in the prayer. Somehow they had fully recovered. The man's splitting headache had also stopped.

In appreciation for helping his family, the man donated a parcel of land in Omoba Phase II, Onitsha for my ministry. That is how I received the first plot of land in the commercial city of Onitsha. The well-fenced land, complete with a gate, was situated in a very expensive area of town. While promising to continue supporting us, he told us we could build our church there. We considered the land too small for the construction of a church.

Therefore, when I received two plots of land at another location, which was not as expensive, but large enough for a church, I had to sell the former to buy the latter.

On the two plots of land, I started Power Chapel Evangelical Church in 1999. All along, I had not set up an actual church. What I was doing was pure evangelism: praying for people, organizing Bible studies, prayer meetings, fellowships and vigils, and conducting family and personal deliverances.

With the church building and full complements of the church offices, the only outstanding item to conclude the all-inclusive church was the erection of permanent quarters for the people of my passion, people with psychiatric problems, commonly referred to as mad persons. That was the stage my ministry had reached before the accident that changed my whole story.

three

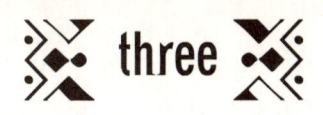

The Accident

Life's challenges continued even after I had founded a thriving church with a large congregation. Curiously, some of the most serious cases—one of which led to my death—originated from my household. The first major case occurred in early July of 2001, barely three years after I established the church.

I was, and have always been, the first-generation breadwinner of my father's large family. That responsibility earned me the heavy burden of caring for my siblings and others. I am also the fourth of mother's eleven children. Therefore, when I eventually built a house, some of my siblings moved in with my immediate family. This was a normal Nigerian practice. However, over time, the atmosphere at home became very tense, due to my wife's regular reports that my brothers didn't like me. I found her accusations strange, and the only rationalization I could come up with was that she wanted her immediate family all to herself. Regardless, she persisted, eventually insisting that I send them away. I found her request very un-African.

Matters came to a head when she narrated a particular encounter. She quoted my younger brother whom I had brought from the village to assist me in the church as saying, "You and your husband will not live to spend the money you are making if you aren't careful."

According to her, my brother threatened, "We will kill your husband, kill your son, drive you away, and inherit this house."

I found that an absolutely horrible accusation for a wife to make. In total disbelief of her story, I ordered her to leave my house. She left with our children the following morning, saying, "I'm going. I'm going to my own parents. I can't stay here and let them kill you and my only son."

She left, and the devil entered with offers that nearly ruined my ministry and my life. I decided to marry a member of my church to fill the void left by Nneka. The woman, the daughter of a retired judge, lived in London. In the heat of the blossoming relationship, I dreamt of handing the church over to my brothers and moving to London to live with the lady and start a church.

THE ACCIDENT

My plans included obtaining a divorce certificate from any court to satisfy the judge's requirement and arranging a quiet wedding. However, the familiar voice always reminded me of God's love for me. On my way back to Onitsha after a crusade in Sokoto, northern Nigeria, I heard an order clearly, "Dan, if you don't bring your wife back home immediately, you will die."

The order came on Monday, but the following day, I discovered that my lawyer had made significant progress in obtaining a divorce certificate. We were set to finalise the arrangement on Wednesday. Surprisingly, as I left home for the lawyer's office that morning, I was prompted by the Holy Spirit to change course. I headed for Aba, where Nneka was living with one of her close relations. In normal African tradition, they would have sought an explanation for sending their daughter away. That day, I wasn't afraid to go to them for my wife.

I arrived in Aba safely and headed straight to their house. As I opened the gate, she saw me. However, unlike in the past when she would have turned cold, she smiled broadly as she stood on the veranda. Even in her simple blouse and skirt and performing house chores, she looked elegant and adorable. When I approached her, she welcomed me, but as I responded, her mood suddenly changed.

She sounded grumpy. "Let me tell you, I heard that

you want to marry a girl in the church. Aren't you ashamed of yourself? Even if you marry two or more wives, I know I'm your only wife."

"Who told you all that?" I quickly tried to defend myself.

She wouldn't respond to my question. Looking broken-hearted, she knelt down before me and pleaded, "I beg you, please forgive me. From what your brothers were doing, I thought they hated you."

"That's all over now." I pulled her up and hugged her. "That's exactly why I'm here. Get the children and let's go out for some snacks."

I had not seen her that happy in a long time.

Shortly after, she joined me with the kids in the car, and we headed for the fast food eatery. I wasn't sure if her people saw me, but I wasn't ready for a lengthy conversation now that I had my wife back.

As we ate the snacks, I promised her we would return to Onitsha to live as husband and wife, without any interference from our respective families. She was so elated she could hardly eat. Still unwilling to see her people, I gave her time to return to their house to pack her property and return to her matrimonial home.

A few moments later, her mood changed again. "How can I be sure you won't throw me out again?"

My response was prompt, "I won't, so go and prepare

THE ACCIDENT

for your return on Friday. I will come and pick you up. It will be faster if you don't tell your people. You can leave them a letter telling them you have returned to your matrimonial home."

She didn't look convinced. I watched her pout and realized I had to sound more convincing. "You know how fast our life is moving, Nneka. The devil is also moving fast to destroy us, so we can't leave any room for him. Friday is even too long." I stood up and carried one of our children out to the car.

Her face broke into a buoyant grin. "Okay, Friday!" she almost shouted.

When I told the story back in Onitsha, both the lawyer and the judge's daughter were disappointed in me, but I didn't care.

The Friday I was to go pick up my wife and children from Aba was another eventful day—another milestone of God's Glory in my life. The day before, my blood brother, called Favour, who was living with me, had seen me bring some money to my Amaimo home. I was going to use it for the development of a property.

My plan was to visit Aba in the afternoon, but my car developed an engine problem, and I couldn't fix it until late in the day. Not willing to risk a night trip with my entire family, I decided to wait until the following day to go to Aba.

At 11 p.m. in my home in Amaimo I received some unusual company. A loud bang on the door startled me.

I heard Favour's voice, "Please open the door."

"Where have you been? Why are you coming home at this time of the night, and why do you want to see me?" I asked, trying to collect my thoughts.

He told me the situation was urgent. However, since he refused to explain exactly what the matter involved, I insisted he wait until the following morning.

At five o'clock the following morning on July 22, 2001, I opened the door and summoned him. A gang of three attackers burst into the room and started pounding me.

"What kind of rubbish is this?" I shouted in desperation. "What's going on?"

They continued to punch me and then suddenly stopped. I took a quick look around and was convinced by the looks on their face that they meant business. They ordered me to sign three cheques for 100,000 Naira each, but I pleaded that the money was for the payment to be made later in the day to a company. I advised them that Favour could back me up on that point.

After hearing that comment, my brother lunged for the money and ordered one of the attackers to shoot me.

THE ACCIDENT

"You people shouldn't forget that he that keepeth Israel neither slumbers nor sleeps," I thundered.

"Devil, who asked you to say that?" my brother shouted back and slapped me.

Suddenly, the man with the pistol shot me. I felt the sharp stabbing pain of knife wounds all over my body. Finally, a knife cut my throat. As I passed out my attackers fled.

By the Grace of God, I didn't die. I was taken to the Umezurike Hospital in Owerri. I had to send for my wife, who was waiting for me at Aba. Despite my pain, I detected a combination of pity and triumph in her wet, red eyes.

She later said, "Didn't I tell you? I told you your brothers were trying to kill you."

I recovered very quickly, and when I was discharged with my neck bandaged, everyone was thankful to God. I promised Nneka that I would not allow anyone to come between us. To further reassure her about the security of our marriage, I took her to see the lady who was working so hard to replace her.

Surprisingly, her family was happy to receive us. The lady confessed she didn't really know how to accept me as her husband. She had been worried about how it would look to marry another woman's husband.

"That was why I insisted you bring a divorce certificate." The retired judge declared, "We thank God for saving you a broken home and saving your life. He always triumphs over the devil."

I was moved to remorse. I reflected on one of the mistakes that shook my life. Indeed, before this all started, I dreamt about the lady and myself, drinking and smoking at a disco club. When I awoke, I asked myself if going to London with this girl meant I would backslide. However, the pressure was already so intense that I felt like finishing what I had started.

That's one of the reasons I never fail to advise people, "The race is not by power, neither is it by might, but by the hand of God upon one's life."

When the dust settled over my shame, I understood the seriousness of God's warning that if I failed to bring back my wife, I would die. The scar on my neck is a daily reminder of temptation's power to ruin and the greater strength of the grace and glory of God in my life.

With my family back and the devil put to shame, I returned to work full-time, doing what God had intended when he saved my life on numerous occasions. From those experiences and the spiritual anointing he has gracefully given me, I owed him the duty to preach his Word. My church continued to grow, and I loved converting unbelievers who were in the devil's stronghold. I organized crusades in communities that worshipped idols. Although they were always stormy encounters, God always triumphed over the idols and set the people free. I became very popular for the physical and spiritual destruction of idols; people even nicknamed me the "Idol Destroyer." However, despite the euphoria, I never forgot the true power behind me—God.

Five months after we promised each other bliss, a major disaster struck in our marriage. Once again, God intervened in a miraculous way that completely changed my life. One weekend, our last son at that time, Ifeanyi, fell ill. On November 26, 2001, Nneka felt the case was serious enough to take the fifteen-month-old boy to the hospital. On that day, I was scheduled to commence a widely-publicised crusade at Mbaise-Umuneoha, in Imo State, and destroy the village deity. Therefore, I decided to take mother and child to the hospital and continue to Mbaise-Umuneoha for the crusade.

The news we received at the Edjor Pediatric hospital near the Ose main market in Onitsha was grim and justified Nneka's insistence that I accompany them. The doctor warned us that Ifeanyi had lost a dangerous amount of blood; he required immediate treatment starting with a blood donation from one of us. Since Nneka was four-months pregnant, I was the obvious choice. For a moment, I felt that wasn't safe for a man planning a three-day crusade, but I believed that God would take control at both ends.

I promptly removed my jacket, rolled up the right sleeve of my shirt, and offered my veins so the nurse could draw a pint of blood for Ifeanyi. It was late in the morning, and I hadn't eaten. Therefore, I heeded the doctor's advice and gulped down a can of malt to Nneka's obvious discomfort. My body language clearly revealed that I was anxious to attend the crusade, and Nneka was visibly incensed. She glowered and avoided looking at my eyes. She spoke very little, only grunting a few angry words. I begged her to let me go, paid the required deposit of 12,000 Naira for the treatment, and left in the early afternoon.

At Mbaise-Umuneoha, the crusade drew a large crowd and didn't end until Wednesday night. I left on Thursday morning pleased with the number of people who had given their lives to Christ. I couldn't wait to break the news to Nneka, whom I always prayed for during the crusades. I was so eager to see her I couldn't even wait to eat in the village. I packed the food, fried chicken and all, into a cooler to enjoy at home with my wife and kids. However, I arrived home later in the day greeted by a gloomy atmosphere.

Nneka wore a heavy frown, but she refused to tell me

Mortuary attendent with Rev. Dan.

Wreckage of Dan's car after the accident.

The doctor who confirmed Dan's death.

Dan's parents.

Mortuary register showing Dan's name.

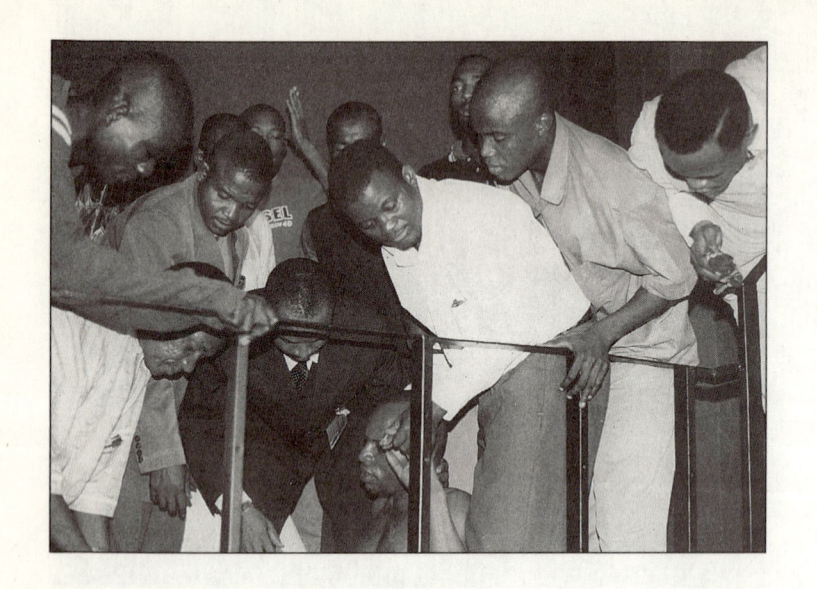

Dan, back to life.

Dan and wife, Nneka.

what was wrong. I knew in the spirit, even at Mbaise-Umuneoha, that Ifeanyi was okay; therefore his health couldn't be blamed for her coldness.

"My dear, the boy is okay. Is anything else the matter?" I pleaded.

"What kind of man of God are you? Are you the only man of God in this country?" She jumped up from where she sat in the living room and moved towards me.

"What else could I have done? I took you to the hospital, paid for the treatment, and even offered my blood."

"What man of God would abandon his wife and son at the hospital?" She cut me short. Nneka, who is heavily built, charged towards me like a tank.

"You have no job, and taking care of our baby is difficult for you to do?"

Wham! She silenced me with a loud slap across the face.

"What?" I shouted in anger. As I raised my hand to retaliate, an inner voice yelled, "Stop!" so I did. I was afraid not only of God but also of the effect of the news on my ministry that the pastor beat his wife.

I stormed into my room and locked the door. I was still fuming, which was also was wrong, so I knelt to pray. I calmed down considerably. However, when she came by later to offer me food, I was in no mood to see her.

"Please, Darling, forgive me, and come enjoy your dinner. Please forgive me. It was the work of the devil," she pleaded from the other side of the door.

"You call it the work of the devil. I don't think he has finished with you," I admonished, keeping my voice as low as possible.

She would not relent. She continued to plead with me, but when I responded with complete silence, she eventually left.

Later that night, I felt so hungry that I sneaked into the kitchen to look for food. All hope of finding food in the cooler I brought home was dashed when I found it empty. All of the rice and fried chicken was gone. That discovery aggravated my hunger even more. In an effort to avoid re-igniting my anger, I decided to return to my room. Although I hadn't eaten the entire day, I didn't have a choice. I tried unsuccessfully to sleep. Thoughts of my father's warning against marrying a lady from Anambra State, "because of their stubbornness," flooded my mind and fanned my anger.

Before daybreak, I refreshed myself and was ready to go to the village to tell my parents that the marriage they initially resisted had finally broken down. I was confident they would support my decision because in our culture it is an abomination for a wife to slap her husband.

I opened my door at five, the following morning. To

THE ACCIDENT

my utter surprise, Nneka was standing at the door, tears flooding her eyes.

She greeted me, "Daddy, good morning," as our eyes met. "Your breakfast is ready. Please forgive me." I greeted her pleas with stony silence.

Ignoring her, I tore through the living room and raced down the stairs to the garage. I had tethered a ram, which had been offered in thanks by a member of the church, near my car. I placed the animal into the trunk and zoomed off to my village.

At the village, I promptly offered the ram to my anxious Dad. He calmed down when I explained that the ram was for their Christmas celebration and that I would bring bags of rice on my next trip. Because it was November, my gift made sense. When I added that I had forgiven my brother, who had attempted to kill me for money, I saw his eyes fill with both surprise and joy.

I later went to visit my mother on the veranda. I gave her some money, returned to my father in the living room to also give him some money, and then I broke the news of my divorce.

"Why now, my son?" My father sat up on the sofa.

When I told him my wife slapped me, he jumped up, fuming. "Abomination, abomination," he shouted as he paced the room.

That drew my mother's attention. I love her so much.

When I saw her breath become more rapid, I knew I had to handle the situation with the utmost care.

"I heard that, I heard it all from where I sat, my son," she slumped onto the sofa beside me. I could hear her breath, and I knew I had to do something. After my tumultuous childhood and all her sacrifices, she felt rewarded by what God was doing in my life; she was averse to anything that would turn back the hands of time.

I told them both that I wanted my wife to stay with them in the village for a year, while I remained in Onitsha to work. They accepted the suggestion very reluctantly, but I suspected they knew the option left them ample opportunity for maneuvering and reconciliation.

I left the village with mixed feelings about the compromise with my mother in particular. Fortunately, Kingsley Eruka, a young man who wanted to accompany me to Onitsha, was present to keep me company on the drive home. Chatting with him provided me much needed relief. In fact, it wasn't until when we arrived on Osuma Street, where my house was located, that I remembered the unresolved problem at home. It was 6:00 p.m. and another tense night was beckoning.

We were a few metres down the steep slope to my house, when something very unexpected happened. The brakes of my Mercedes Benz 230 suddenly failed, sending us barreling uncontrollably down the road, which bordered a big, deep ditch. Luckily, some pillars had been erected at the edges of the valley as safety reminders of the monstrous valley. At a point where I had to negotiate a sharp bend, I lost control of the car and crashed into one of the concrete pillars.

The impact was so severe that Kingsley lunged forward and broke the windshield with his head. He wasn't wearing a seat belt. Neither was I, so my ribs had smashed into the steering wheel, forcing a lungful of air from my mouth. I found it almost impossible to breathe. My chest cavity had obviously collapsed, and when I started vomiting blood, fear overwhelmed me!

Neighbours who had heard the noise of the accident, and my cry for help, forced the doors open and rushed me to the nearest hospital. We made the journey in a neighbour's Mercedes Benz to St. Charles Borromeo Hospital, a Catholic hospital in Onitsha, at about 7:00 p.m.

The doctors started work on me promptly at the casualty ward. With my entire body in pain, I found it very difficult to breathe. They inserted an IV into my arm and tried to insert a catheter, but the pain was excruciating. I tried to scream, but the words died in my mouth. All I needed was the sweet breath of air into my lungs. I was only able to take shallow, infrequent breaths, shaking my hope for survival.

I finally summoned all my strength and asked that

my wife be brought to see me immediately. Before she arrived, I had a practical encounter with death. An inner voice kept advising me, "Why are you subjecting yourself to all this pain? Why are you punishing yourself? If you give up now, all the pain will disappear, and you will be welcomed into a blissful world where there is no pain, only joy."

I knew the voice did not belong to God. I countered it with the quote the invisible pastor taught me when I had the tetanus attack in early childhood, "I have not finished the work God sent me to do, so why should I die? I will not die!"

The mischievous voice would not be so easily defeated. The voice appeared for the second time when the pain became unbearable. However, this time the voice was soothing. By the time it came the third time, it was so convincing that I finally accepted it.

I told myself, "Yes I will die." Immediately after making the decision, all my pain disappeared, and I could breathe normally again. Then I asked, "Where is my wife?" in a strong voice that must have surprised the nurses.

The nurses told me she was on her way. At that, I started a parting prayer, which alarmed the members of my church surrounding me. They shouted my name to stop the prayer and countered it with a prayer of life.

When the nurses urged them to leave me alone, I prayed again.

During the prayer, I remembered that I had been involved in an accident. I knew I had pain all over, but I experienced a little relief by praying, "Oh God, forgive me all my sins and cleanse me with the blood of Jesus. Count me worthy please. If I die, accept my soul—"

At that moment, Nneka burst into the ward and countered, "You will not die in the name of Jesus." She started screaming for divine help, as the nurses tried to calm her. I was quiet once again. I didn't know where she went, but moments later, she returned to my bedside and declared, "We are leaving here, Daddy." I was too weak to argue and couldn't ask questions, as she stormed out again.

Upon her return, she told my church members that the doctor had refused to discharge me unless she signed an undertaking. With the support of the church members, she finally signed the undertaking and paid the bill I had incurred. They then loaded me into a waiting ambulance, with Nneka seated beside me.

As I later learned, we left the hospital for Owerri at about 9:00 p.m. Looking back today, it still amazes me that my wife would take me that far to continue treatment given my physical condition. From that point on, she was to blame for any incident. However, I learned from my experience with God, that some of the amazing things he has done in people's lives follow no logical sequence. In human weakness, God's strength is made perfect.

Shortly after the ambulance left the hospital, I felt the pain return in full force, strong enough to make me wonder why I had been discharged. The speed of the ambulance on the bumpy road made my body shake, but Nneka did all she could to hold me steady.

I felt death approaching. Somewhere along the route, which I later learned was near Ihiala, I felt I wouldn't survive the trip. With the little strength I could muster, I began to advise her how to run the home and relate to the members of my family and the church, reminding her where I kept all the vital documents of my properties.

My weak state denied me a clear perception of her reaction so I continued to ramble. "God has blessed us. We have already built our own house at the village, and we have a lot of material things for you and the children. We have two boys and one girl and you're pregnant."

"No," I heard her shout. "I reject it in the name of Jesus!"

However, at that point, I had expended my last burst of energy. I shut my mouth and closed my eyes, insensitive to my physical environment.

I had heard about it and preached it, so I knew I was in the spiritual world upon the arrival of two angels in the ambulance. All white, with wings, they looked like the angels you often see in paintings, but I was still afraid because those paintings didn't provide enough detail. The angels looked huge and their eyes were completely white, with no pupils. They had white hair and wore long white gowns which clung tightly to their skin. I call them gowns, because the angels had the stature of humans, and the irremovable garments seemed to cover their nakedness. Their long gowns reached the floor. I confess I couldn't see their footwear. Their faces were the same colour as their white garments. It is difficult to determine whether the garment stretched that far or whether it actually formed part of their skin. Although they appeared to be men in my opinion, perhaps because of my own sex, it was impossible to definitely determine their sex. After gazing in amazement at the angels, I suddenly felt afraid and wanted to shout.

"Shsssh!" One of them raised his hand to his lips to silence me.

With that gesture, my power of speech was taken from me. The angels bent over and gently lifted me in their palms. As they started to move, I quickly turned my head to look back at my wife. I watched her shaking my badly bruised and bloody body in an attempt to revive me, tears streaming down her cheeks. However, the body in the hands of the angels was very fresh and intact with no wounds. My breathing was also normal. Obviously,

Nneka was unaware of what was happening. I tried to say something to her, but I couldn't speak.

As if they had allowed me only one final glimpse of my wife, we immediately disappeared from the ambulance. We exited in the same manner they arrived, with no doors opening or shutting and no breaking of metal. We simply disappeared.

From this point on, my story flows along two separate lines until they finally converge. From here, the story on Earth is better told by the woman who went through all the pain, loss, humiliation, self-judgment regarding murder and obvious poor decisions, which turned out to manifest the power of God.

four

Nneka's Testimony

As an African, I knew that I had caused an abomination when I slapped my husband. As a Christian, I also couldn't justify my actions. He attended a crusade, and I knew it. I wanted him to show the love and care other men show their wives and sick children when Ifeanyi was in the hospital. However, he went to work for God, and I knew it. Therefore, wherever he had gone that early morning, I was accountable for his safety before God and man.

By midday, my heart began to beat wildly as if I had run a long distance. The premonition was too strong to bear because of my guilt. I was afraid he had returned to his village to initiate a divorce, but I was more concerned about his safety. I commenced emergency prayers,

"God, please touch him anywhere he goes, and let him come back so that he will know that I have changed." I even bought a new bedspread at the market. I washed his room and tidied everything. I did all the things I knew would make him happy.

In trepidation, I waited and prayed until 4:00 p.m., but there was no sign of him. The situation was made worse by the fact that I was unable to seek advice from anyone. I had to make sure no one discovered what had transpired in a pastor's family.

I stayed rooted in our duplex, expecting to see him walk in at any second. Six p.m. arrived, with no sign of him. I looked out the windows to see groups of people hanging around and speaking in hushed tones. Some of them were pointing at our duplex, but I was so scared I didn't want to know what had attracted them. My wish was that my husband, who hadn't eaten, would at least return home for his dinner.

While I was pondering all the possibilities that could have kept him so late, I heard one of the boys outside shout, "Oh, that pastor had an accident, and he died."

The moment I heard this, I became frantic. I sprinted downstairs and out into the crowd.

"Come back, it's not your husband, it's not a pastor!" I heard people shouting and running after me on the Osuma road.

At one point, I tumbled and fell. I remembered falling and being lifted up, but I have no recollection of exactly what happened and how we arrived back at the house.

A while later I started hearing voices, many people talking at the same time. "Oh, she's pregnant; go and buy milk and a malt drink, mix them, and give it to her. Everybody get out. Go away; go away." In the cacophony of voices, I felt myself regaining consciousness. I saw groups of people, men and women, old and young, all trying to calm me down. "We were talking about the other pastor who lives in the house over there. It's not your husband. If it were your husband, we would certainly tell you," one of them said. Despite their attempt to console me, my spirit was telling me it was my husband. The large crowd of people just confirmed my suspicions. I kept flashing back to our quarrel the previous night, making me feel guilty for causing whatever had happened to him.

The confusion and cover-ups were clarified when an elderly man entered the room. He broke the news that my husband had been involved in an accident, but he was alive and wanted to see me. I accompanied the man to his car and headed to the hospital.

To date, I don't know how I survived my first sight of him. He was lying naked with all kinds of tubes inserted into his nose and private parts. He was breathing with extreme difficulty, and he was clearly fighting to survive. I told myself that the situation was beyond me, and I dashed into the doctor's room to inquire what was happening.

He replied, "We have been giving him treatment, but he is responding very gradually. You should pray for his recovery."

At that pronouncement, I believed he had very little hope of recovery if he remained at that hospital. I lost confidence in the hospital and decided to move him, but the doctor insisted I write an undertaking to assume responsibility for whatever happened to him. I accepted the condition and the additional responsibility. I signed the undertaking and paid the bill he had incurred. With the assistance of the many people present, including our church members, we carried him to the ambulance out front.

He had been successfully treated at the Umezurike Hospital in Owerri when his brother attacked him months earlier. However, I don't know what gave me the faith to risk the more than 100-kilometre distance with a man who was so weak. My decision was definitely instinctive.

I rode with him in the ambulance while some church members accompanied us in front. The ambulance tore through the streets of Onitsha towards Owerri at top speed, with sirens blaring.

My husband remained quiet and was breathing slowly, until he began to speak several minutes into the journey.

He called out to me and told me not to worry if he died because he always said he would die young. He reminded me that if I recalled his background, the dramatic turnaround, how God had used him mightily, and the growth of his ministry, this just confirmed what he had always said.

Terrified, I began to oppose and reject the spirit of death, stating, "Devil, you can't kill him. I reject you in the name of Jesus. I cast you out!"

I continued to pray in the ambulance and massage him until I noticed he had completely stopped breathing. I felt his pulse, but there wasn't one. At that point, I screamed, "God, that isn't my covenant with you this year."

In order to restore peace of mind at that terrible moment, I meditated on a passage from Isaiah, which says, "Arise, shine for your light has come, and the glory of the Lord rises upon you" (Isaiah 60:1). I took that as God's promise, which also implied that I shouldn't experience violence in my home again, and that my home shall be called the city of the Lord.

For that reason, I held my husband's cold hand and prayed, "God, no, this is not what you told me at the beginning of this year. You spoke clearly to me, God." (At the beginning of the year, I had begged God to spare me another violence in our home because of an attack on my husband, during which his brother tried to kill him.)

At that point, we could only go one way, so I told the driver to continue speeding while I continued praying. I had lost track of time, but we eventually reached Umezurike Hospital.

As soon as the ambulance stopped, I jumped out and screamed for help. A nurse promptly arrived, as I shouted, "It's an accident! It's an accident!"

She looked at my husband, examined his pulse, and then closed his eyelids and pronounced the verdict that sent me sprawling on the floor.

"He's dead. Do you want me to call the mortuary attendant?" she asked me in a very faint voice.

At the mention of death, I jumped up. "He isn't dead. I reject it. His life has been saved in this hospital before. Call the doctor. Call the doctor!"

"Madam, I know what I'm saying." The cold night seemed to freeze her words.

"Okay, I'll try another hospital," I screamed and jumped back into the ambulance. I ordered the driver to drive to another private hospital, since public hospitals were on strike at the time.

We arrived at St. Eunice Clinic, the doctor, Jossy Anuebunisa, performed a quick examination and pronounced the same verdict—dead. He advised me he had been dead for a while, and he recommended a mortuary. I declined the offer, choosing to let the father in Amaimo, who lived almost thirty minutes away, see him first. Therefore, we went to Amaimo that night.

I jumped out as soon as the ambulance parked at the entrance of the compound. I shouted, "God, I'm in trouble!" and slumped to the ground. My legs could no longer carry me.

The shout brought my father-in-law scrambling out into the eerie night. "What is it?"

"It's my husband, it's my husband. He died in an accident." I was tearing at my hair and pacing frantically.

The news didn't sink in right away, perhaps because he had seen his son earlier that day. However, a few moments later, he screamed, "My God! When did it happen?"

He didn't wait for my answer; he looked at the body in the ambulance and hurried to his room. "He's dead, but crying will attract too many people and stop us from what we must do," he declared firmly as he moved towards me. "Try and hold yourself together so we can take him to the Ikeduru Community Hospital mortuary. It's not far from here. If the mortician also pronounces him dead, we can leave him in the mortuary there."

The mortician, Mr. Barlington Manu, checked to ensure he was really dead, and then handed us a form to complete. Hardened by his job, Manu appeared stoned-faced and surprisingly unsympathetic. He recorded our details in a register and transported the body into a morgue fringed by a maize farm. Because the village mortuary had no cold storage facilities, Manu injected some chemicals into the body and prepared it for embalming the following morning. Many dead bodies filled the room, all neatly packed on cement slabs. With the support of his son, Manu laid the body on top of three slabs in a row at the far end of the mortuary.

The many corpses I saw convinced me beyond a doubt that my husband, whose death I must have caused, had joined the dead. I felt bitter inside. My head was heavy, and I was unable to think clearly.

When I returned home that night, sympathizers, especially women, swarmed around me. I missed my mother-in-law, who I was told had traveled to Ufuma to visit her first daughter who was sick. Food and sleep were out of the question. Later that night, my father-in-law called me to his room. He told me we should return to Onitsha at daybreak to tell church members the news and to "put the things in our house together." So we left for Onitsha that morning. I tried to control my emotions, but they remained bottled up, ready to erupt at any second.

When we arrived at the Onitsha home, I began to sense what other losses I was to endure when my father-in-law told me he didn't want anything removed from the house. He took money from me to get my husband's elder brother who lived on the outskirts of town.

I was in the living room, with sympathizers milling around me, when they returned. In the presence of the sympathizers, he told me there was no time for protocol. He advised me to pack my belongings and get my children to head for the village where I would be staying.

I found that unacceptable given that my husband had not even been buried. I could hear some of our church members whisper that my in-laws were out to take over my husband's property.

The chairman of the church, Brother Joseph Orhakute, protested this decision. He reminded my in-laws that my husband was the General Overseer of our church and that I should remain with the other members of the congregation during the burial arrangements.

Unfortunately, my in-laws felt otherwise, insisting that I be treated like any other widow, and not as a pastor's wife. I knew that meant I might even be forced to participate in some rituals.

As they argued, my father-in-law told the landlord that I wasn't allowed to remove any item from the house without his direct permission.

"Trouble!" I muttered, and rationalised that perhaps I deserved that for sending my husband to his death by slapping him. I sat, praying quietly.

In spite of the arguments made by our church members, I was dragged back to the village to remain close to my husband. We got back on Saturday night, but I wasn't in the mood for a pity party. I had an inexplicably strong conviction that my husband wasn't dead.

When it was time to sleep, I realized that I had been struck by insomnia. I tried to relax, hoping that sleep would eventually come to energise me for my ordeal. I finally dozed off, straight into a dream in which I saw my husband walk straight towards me wearing the same clothes he wore on the day of the accident.

"So Baby,"—he always called me that when he was in a good mood—"are you here enjoying yourself? So you abandoned me in the room of the dead. Come and get me immediately because I'm not dead."

Immediately after he finished speaking, he turned his back, and I woke up startled. I started crying, "My husband isn't dead! He's not dead!"

My cries woke everybody up. The many women surrounding me began to console me. Even my father-in-law came out from his room to join them. He told me that my husband would continue appearing to me for some time because he had died prematurely.

When I calmed down, a Bible verse from Hebrews 11:35 flooded my memory and rang in my ears. "Women received their loved ones back again from death."

The more I recited the verse and prayed, the more I had faith that my husband would return home alive.

I told myself if it were God who was speaking to my heart, it would come to pass because the word of God is infallible. I started crying again. That same night, I told my worried father-in-law that the following morning I would remove my husband from the mortuary and take him to the location where Reinhard Bonnke was holding a programme in Onitsha. That had become necessary because the mortician had sent a message on Saturday, advising me that some spiritual forces kept singing hymns in the compound and were making his work difficult. He warned me that if my husband weren't removed, he would meet force with force. (See the quotes on the last page of this book.)

I had seen the poster of the auditorium-opening ceremony of the Grace of God church in Onitsha by Reinhard Bonnke, but I never planned to attend. That night, however, I felt that I had a problem big enough to attend the ceremony, where the anointing of God would be on display.

My father-in-law promptly rejected the proposal, arguing that I was planning to use his son for a ritual. He warned me that if my plan failed, upon my return to the village, they would bury my husband like a fowl. It would be clear that I killed him. Remaining strong in faith, I was stubborn, and we argued until daybreak.

At exactly 6:00 a.m., my father-in-law came to remind

me that he was a pastor who had prayed for a dead woman to come back to life shortly after she died. Perhaps he could perform the same feat.

I knew he was a pastor who backslid many years ago. However, he insisted he would pray for my husband. He said he would also hit his forehead seven times with a copy of the Bible as he called my husband's name and that would raise him from the dead. I hated to annoy God over a promise he had so firmly laid in my heart, but there was no stopping my father in-law.

At the mortuary that morning, I stood back and watched him perform his "miracle." Although it failed, I retained hope for my option. Therefore, when he emerged sweating in the early morning sun to listen to my proposal again, I felt lifted by the Lord.

He asked me if I knew anybody who could help us. I assured him my spirit convinced me that I should take him to Reinhardt Bonnke's programme so that he could come back to life. Besides, my husband had told me that he wasn't dead. I have a gift for revelation from God. Every revelation he has given me has come to pass. For example, before his brother attacked him, I foresaw the incident and warned him about it.

Determined to meet Bonnke in Onitsha, I made frantic preparations that Sunday morning, after my father in-law failed to perform a miracle. High police curiosity over the increase in local ritual killings necessitated that we dress the body as if we were attending a burial. This would save us undue questioning by the police over the approximately two-hour journey to Onitsha. We placed the body in a coffin provided by my father-in-law and shut the lid.

I was filled with hope, until we arrived at the outskirts of Onitsha, where the devil struck. I slumped into the quicksand of doubt and unbelief. From my experience with the scriptures, I knew that this often happens to people when they're about to receive a miracle, but I couldn't avoid it.

An inner voice started asking me questions such as, "Are you sure it will work and your husband will come back to life? You are a stubborn woman, why can't you accept that he's dead? How are you even sure that Bonnke hasn't left?"

At the last question, I yelled at the driver to park the ambulance. I hopped down to ask passers-by if Bonnke were still in town. The answer from all three people was affirmative. Bonnke was still at the venue of the auditorium-dedication ceremony at the Government Reservation Area in Onitsha. Even with such assurances, I still had to battle with the devil; the cloud of doubt had not yet cleared.

I said a short prayer and jumped into the ambulance. "Driver, you will only stop when I tell you to stop. Turn on the warning siren and move," I ordered the driver.

"Yes, Madam," he agreed, as he zoomed off.

When we finally arrived at the hilltop location of the church, we were greeted by a large assembly of cars and security men, policemen, and soldiers, on a freshly cleared stretch of land down the slope. To ensure that we attracted the desired attention, I ordered the driver to enter the compound of the church by the closest gate. Our audacity obviously infuriated the security men, but by then I had rid myself of all fear and doubt.

As soon as the ambulance stopped, I jumped out and started screaming, "My husband is a pastor. Please come and help me. He isn't dead; he's not dead! He only had an accident!"

Angered, some of the security men descended on me, flogging me with canes, and pushing me away.

"Woman, why are you here? Do you think this place is a cemetery? Who told you to come? Why did you bring your dead husband here? You evil people, you came here to harm Bonnke!" some of them shouted.

They didn't spare the driver either. Once they started to beat him, he abandoned the ambulance, and fled on foot.

They chased him and finally caught up with him, leading him back to the ambulance. Due to the extreme pressure of the situation, and the beating he had just endured, he forgot to shut the back door. As he drove away, the casket jutted out, causing the security men to run back. I rushed to push the casket back in, and I secured the door, amid curses and abuse from the security guards. They ordered us back into the parking lot, but I ran back to the gate of the church, still shouting for help.

When they started to whip me again, I decided grab any of them I could reach just like a mad woman. My strategy worked. The men I held freed themselves and quickly retreated. I continued doing this, until one of the soldiers called out to me, "Madam, what did you say happened to your husband?" He hushed his colleagues into silence so he could hear me.

I told my story quickly between sobs, and I could tell the soldier was moved. "But you should have told the white man before bringing a dead man here," he stated in a sympathetic voice. "Do you know the General Overseer of the church, Reverend Paul Nwachukwu, or any senior member? Are you sure they will allow a dead body in the church at such an occasion?"

I told him that I didn't know anybody there, but I sincerely believed that the anointing of God at a gathering that strong could produce a miracle.

He excused me to tell the head of the church my story, and he quickly returned with the good news that the head of the church was sending his own son, Pastor Paul Jr., to attend to me. I breathed a sigh of relief and said a short prayer.

Shortly after they heard the news, Paul Jr. and some other pastors of the church asked me why I had transported a corpse all the way from Owerri on such an occasion.

"Faith and the high anointing at this particular occasion." I ended my explanation on a strong note.

Paul Jr. didn't talk much. He told me he needed to tell his Dad. He returned shortly after, to tell me we had Dr. Nwachukwu's permission to take the body into the building.

By then the soldiers had become my sympathizers. They carried the body from the casket into the basement of the building, which served as the children's department. Then they laid him gently on his back on a table.

five

I Saw Heaven

From the ambulance, the two angels carried me into the clouds. Like aeroplanes in steep ascent, we passed through layer upon layer of clouds. Unlike my hours of pain and anguish spent in the hospital bed and in the ambulance, I felt healthy and breathed normally, even though I didn't know where we were going. Curiously, even though the angels never spoke to me, I felt absolutely no fear.

At one point during our flight through the clouds, the angels stopped. They let me down to stand, and then disappeared. I was left standing (or rather floating since my feet weren't actually touching anything). Although I was surrounded by clouds that appeared to be structures, they weren't tangible. All around me were sheets of white clouds. They seemed so close. Yet just like the horizon, they couldn't be touched. I stood there with my hands folded behind me, feeling no pain and no fear. I had no idea what to anticipate next. I don't remember if I was wearing anything. Indeed, I had lost any sense of self-appreciation, or even thoughts of the world I had recently left behind.

Suddenly, just as a feeling of being stranded invaded my thoughts, I noticed a lone angel appear from the clouds. He didn't appear to be walking, because a split second later, he was standing before me. Although he had the physical features of the angels who spirited me away from the ambulance, he was so huge and tall he made me wonder how two angels could even fit into the ambulance.

"Dan, are you worried about Goodness and Mercy?" he asked.

My response was muted, because I had either lost my power of speech or I didn't know what to say. Regardless, deep in my heart, I was pleased to see him.

"Dan," his voice was very soothing, "I'm talking about the two angels that brought you here. The one on your right represents goodness, and the one on your left represents mercy. They are meant to follow you every day of your life. When you die, they will bring you back here along with your records. For now, don't be worried about them. You won't see them around here anymore."

"Come with me to the Palace," he beckoned. As soon as he said that, we were transported to another environment. The beauty of this new place is indescribable. White clouds splendidly decorated everywhere. I didn't see any building or any roads. All I saw were pure white clouds! This place was almost exactly like the place we had just vacated. The only difference was that I saw a large crowd of people here. They had eyes, hair, and garments just like the angels. However, they had no wings and they were smaller than the angels. In fact, the people were the same size as human beings, but they all had one colour—white. They were singing a worship song, and they didn't pay any attention to us; they just sang away mellifluously.

As I stood there gazing at the beauty before me, questions flooded my mind. Where was this magnificent place? The angel answered my question immediately.

"Dan, welcome to Paradise."

He never said anything further, allowing me to take in as much of the heavenly place as I pleased. I observed that all the people in the celestial palace appeared ageless and looked alike, except for one man in the centre. He had a glittering silvery white hair and beard. He appeared elderly, which contrasted visibly with the fresher, younger look of everyone else. Knowing that I was in Paradise, I presumed I had just seen God. However, I was wrong.

As soon as the thought came to mind, the angel turned to me and declared, "Dan, the elderly man over there is Father Abraham, not God. The people you see around him are all the children of God who have died in the world. They are now worshipping God in the bosom of Father Abraham."

The method of communication with the angel was silent. Neither of us spoke a word. As soon as a thought or question came to my mind, he answered it instantly without my saying a word.

All of the children of God were singing gloriously with one voice, their gaze focused on a particular spot in the cloud above. The cloud covered them so completely that you could almost imagine being able to reach out and touch it. Out of that cloud radiated a light so bright that I couldn't look at it a second time. Throughout our entire time there, the worshipping children of God remained focused on that light. Their concentrated attention on that bright light didn't affect their body movement during worship. When they wanted to bow, they raised their hands and then bowed simultaneously. The uniformity was perfect. They could bend, bow, and straighten up in any position or direction. However, nothing stopped them from gazing into the light.

Their enduring attention on that light and their enamouring melody motivated me to take another look at the light, but I couldn't. My spirit had already started singing with them, even though I didn't understand the language in which they sang. I felt uplifted by the melody, and I wanted to join them.

Just then the angel warned me, "Dan, don't go in there! Let's go, I have a lot more to show you. I am taking you to the Mansion that Jesus promised his people." For the first time, he told me our destination but wouldn't allow me enough time to process the information. "The Mansion is ready but the saints are not." I could read the pain with which the angel made that statement. Before he completed the sentence, we found ourselves on another plane. The beauty of what I saw was awesome. As I tried to picture what it could be, right there before my own eyes, was an unimaginable, indescribable splendour! I was transfixed by the grandeur! *So this is the heavenly mansion, that mansion that my Lord Jesus promised me!* I mused.

I have had the privilege of travelling to many parts of the world, especially after I came back to life. However, I have never come across anything comparable to the heavenly mansion. The structure was faultless and infinite, rising high into the sky as far as I could see. The endless, snow-white clouds covered the building's details. I noticed something amazing about the mansion, that it appeared to be continually rotating on an invisible axial plane.

I noticed a continual movement from whatever angle I watched. Once I started to pay more attention to the details of the imposing mansion, I noticed other marvels. There were no indications of the materials used in the construction, and I had no idea of the building's dimensions. The mansion radiated a glittering light that gave the impression of a glass background, but it was not glass. I couldn't touch it to know if it was soft or hard, and I was unable to enter so I could feel it. I just watched in amazement! I never saw any men or women; everywhere remained empty and quiet.

Satisfied that I had seen enough, the angel said again, "Dan, you can see that the Mansion is completed, but the saints are not ready. Welcome to Heaven!" Instantly, the melodious, angelic voices I had heard in Paradise resumed. This sound was accompanied by a harmonious clapping of hands that bewildered me. Unlike in Paradise, I didn't see anybody here. However, the voices, songs and the clapping were all the same in rhythm and tenor. From where was this worship coming?

The angel came to my rescue, as usual. "Dan, don't worry about the worship songs in the air. The flowers are singing."

Flowers! I saw them, but I never realized they were flowers. There was nothing green about them. Their golden colour might have deceived me for I never saw plants with such magnificent splendour. Every part of the plants, including their leaves, was the colour of gold.

Pointing for the first time at the luscious, royal beauty, he said, "Look at them. Can you see how they praise God?"

Oh, yes! It was obvious that the flowers were in worship. The opening and closing, hugging and untangling of the leaves synchronized with the sound of clapping.

The angel declared, "Time to go, Dan. I have one more place to show you!"

My next experience was in total contrast to the previous ones. Paradise was an indescribable beauty of endless glory. When we got there, I saw it. The Mansion was the peak of it all—the heavenly abode!

As soon as the angel stated, "Time to go," the words appeared before us, boldly written, *Welcome to the Gates of Hell*.

But I didn't see any gate. This inscription was not written in any language that I could decipher. Like the Paradise experience when I participated in the angelic choruses using my mind, my heart read this inscription in a language I could understand. It wasn't physical. There was something unusual about this place. It was bland and limitless, sealed from top to base. It looked like a wall or vault, although it wasn't. I couldn't detect an opening of any kind. I began to wonder how it functioned.

As I pondered this, the angel once again startled me. He suddenly raised his right hand and pulled effortlessly. Though I was standing right beside him, I didn't see him touch anything. However, as soon as he made the gesture, the sound of the gate opening was unmistakable. I heard anguished yelling, howling, and scowling so deafening that I plugged my ears with my thumbs. It didn't help. I tried to shut my eyes, but that was also ineffective.

When I opened my eyes, I discovered that the place was enveloped in darkness. I wished I could see the inhabitants of Hell, to know the details of their sex, age, and nationality. That wish was instantly granted as the angel provided illumination into the mansion of horror. The building was so large that I couldn't even fathom where it ended. I saw men and women in their physical human form. Although they retained their earthly skin colour, they all looked shrunken and appeared to be suffering from hunger, thirst, and pain. As I watched the intimidating wave of anguish, more people were hurled in with the others. Fresh as in their earthly life, they arrived screaming and wailing.

One striking attitude of these inhabitants of Hell distinguished them from the Saints in Paradise. In the

Paradise scene, the Saints didn't pay us any attention, as if our presence distracted them from their worship. On the other hand, here in Hell the people close to where we stood continued shouting and focusing on me in a manner that indicated they couldn't even see the angel.

The angel's illumination provided me the opportunity to recognise some people I knew very well in their earthly life. Some people were dressed in military camouflage, some wore traditional attire, and some even were dressed like pastors. They were all crying, screaming, and shouting from a distance, begging me to help them. Surprisingly, they never called the angel. I distinctly overheard a pastor who identified himself and his offence as misappropriating church funds. Before he could finish shouting how he planned on refunding the money, an unseen force seized him and flung him aside.

I watched people's bodies continuously dismember, yet the affected persons didn't die. Instead, a kind of regeneration occurred immediately. A mighty force would take hold of the head, the owner would scream and wail painfully, and moments later, the head would fall off the neck. The hands, thighs, and legs, would all undergo a similar process of dismemberment. Just when you were about to conclude that the person was saved from further agony, there would be an immediate, imperceptible reconnection of all the dismembered body parts. The entire process would start all over again!

Then the Angel asked, "Dan, do you know why the process has to start all over again?"

I replied that I didn't know why.

He said, "Because this place is eternity. These people can't die, and they can't change. The process you are watching will continue forever and ever."

It was my turn to offer a shrill shout. I thought I had experienced enough, but apparently not yet. My hollering brought me face-to-face with another set of people with a completely different punishment! Here, men and women were frantically ripping off their own private parts. They screamed and wailed as they pulled and tore at themselves. As they carried on painfully, their organs experienced continual reconnection. As with the first scene, this horrible scene of torture and anguish was being re-enacted over and over.

Once again, the Angel offered an explanation. "Dan, this group is made up of idolaters, fornicators, and adulterers. They practised harlotry, which is why they want to remove the very thing that brought them here. Unfortunately, it's too late now."

I witnessed many other types of punishment that were too horrendous to recount. I watched people eating their own flesh as they whimpered in pain. Incessantly, they would bite off a piece of their flesh and then spit it out. Not one of these poor individuals shed a single drop of blood! According to the Angel, these were the witches and wizards who specialised in devouring human flesh and feasting on human blood while on Earth.

"They will forever continue to reap what they once sowed," remarked the Angel.

I encountered yet another group of people. For the first time since I began my experience of the life beyond, I noticed what looked like soil, the type we have here on Earth. All of a sudden, the ground broke wide open and swallowed several people. However, a disagreement seemed to be taking place. Instantly, they would be pulled out again, completely covered in an awful dust that they appeared to chew! These people took many people's lives.

"They will go on burying themselves and eating the land forever and ever," the Angel explained.

While the Angel spoke, more and more people were being hurled in to the mix. At that point, an inexplicable fear overcame me. I began to consider the state of the people being constantly thrown into the smouldering anguish of Hell.

In that instant, the angel said to me, "Dan, Hell has enlarged its coast; it has mobilized its agents on Earth to fill it."

I watched the latest batch of people who had just arrived. As I spotted many who had been involved in killing, the Angel drove a death-knell to my soul, when he turned his attention to me!

"Dan, if your record were to be concluded right now, you would certainly spend your eternity here!"

For the first time, I turned and faced him. I screamed, declaring my innocence, but he turned his back on me.

When I finished, he turned and faced me with a frown. He had always been friendly up until now so his frown compounded my fear.

Before he judged me, he quoted what the Scripture says about Hell in Isaiah 5:14. Then in a harsh voice, for the very first time, he chastised me, "Dan, stop making those claims, and never ever speak to me that way!" Then he added, "This is why the judgment will start from the house of God. For those who don't believe, they are condemned already, and a condemned person has no judgment. But for those that believe, a new life is given to them. They must give account of that new life. Dan, we judge you."

The Angel never used "I" but rather "we."

He raised his hand, and a Bible appeared. He continued, "Dan, we judge you from the words of Jesus Christ."

He read from Matthew 5:21–24. "Did you know that

being a pastor is a sacrifice and that sacrifice cannot be acceptable when you have something against your neighbour?" He then quoted Mark 11:25–26 and read out my judgment, "Dan, what claim are you making about being a child of God? Do you not know that you must reap what you sow? If you sow unforgiveness, you must reap unforgiveness. Dan, on that Thursday night when your wife slapped you, you planned evil against her in your heart. She knocked on your door at midnight begging you to forgive her, but you refused to open the door. In the morning, you left home still angry, without accepting her apologies. On your way back, you had an accident. You only asked God to forgive you when you believed you were going to die. Dan that last prayer of yours was unacceptable because you were unable to forgive your wife."

While the judgment was being read to me, I accepted every bit of it in my heart, urging the Angel to continue. Everything he spoke was the truth, and like a child, I accepted it all. He told me that the new life in Christ was given to us all in the spirit of forgiveness. Therefore, we all ought to live that life in forgiveness.

Emphasizing that we reap what we sow, he declared with finality, "Dan, this place is your portion."

As soon as he concluded his pronouncement, I broke into a strident scream. I felt that the unseen power that had been propelling the multitude into hell would hurl me in with them. I closed my eyes and continued screaming, "Oh, is this how I have destroyed my own soul?" I didn't believe that my wife was responsible for that judgment. I didn't even remember her, even though her "case" was used to determine my judgment and then closed. I didn't remember my children either. In fact, I remembered nothing: the cars, the house, or the projects. Absolutely nothing.

As I continued to wail about my misfortune, I came to realise that God isn't interested in our self-justification. Remember that I attended a crusade to destroy a family deity, conduct deliverance for the family, pray for them, and then lead them to Christ? Remember also that I had donated my blood? Look at my life in the ministry, the number of people I successfully delivered to Christ and released from their demonic stranglehold. All of these arguments didn't count in my favour. I went on bemoaning my misfortune in my own way of crying. To my amazement, I discovered that I had not been thrown into Hell.

The angel then came close to me, placed his right hand on my shoulder and said, "Dan, stop crying. We have decided to send you back to the world, for the request of the rich man is granted to this generation as a last warning." He immediately touched me again, and suddenly I forgot everything about Hell and its horrible tortures. I can't say if he closed the Gates of Hell in the same manner that he opened them. All I knew is that we were on a high hill that was resplendently serene and covered in an enchanting snow-white colour. This place was so remarkably different from the reprehensibly riotous and suffocating atmosphere of Hell!

While we stood there, adoration songs rendered in the most angelic and harmonious voices filled the air. Then the Angel directed my gaze to an opening on the side of the hill. The space was black and deep. Through it, we could see a large crowd of people in the distance.

As we descended into the opening, I couldn't see the Angel any longer. The opening was so frighteningly dark that I started screaming again. Was I returning to Hell? I screamed and screamed until I landed alive in the basement of the Cathedral of Grace of God Mission in Onitsha.

six

To Heaven and Back

Meanwhile, Nneka's ordeal in the church continued. After my husband's body was laid on the table, I became more conscious of my environment. I began to see the four other people, including my in-laws, who had come with me from Amaimo.

The small hall was crammed with curious onlookers, with the pastors led by Paul Jr., Barth Nkwando, Lawrence Onyeka and Luke Ibekwe, praying ceaselessly for him. I joined them in silent prayer. I later heard that Bonnke had stated during the unveiling of the plaque, "What God will do today in this place, the whole world will hear." I believed his words were a prophecy for me.

Although the news of the dead body in the Cathedral had spread at the high table of the ceremony, Bonnke never came down to the children's department to pray for my husband. I still believed the entire building had been electrified with enough anointing to bring my husband back to life.

The torrent of prayers was so powerful that I could feel my spirit move inside me. The torrent had continued for many minutes, and I suddenly noticed my husband draw a long breath, followed by a few short bursts.

"Hallelujah!" I jumped with joy as did many of the onlookers. But the pastors weren't distracted. They promptly stripped him to his waist and began to massage his body, which was as stiff as a board.

News of my husband breathing again broke in the sanctuary and the parking lot, creating pandemonium, which became a problem to manage. Ignoring the distractions, the pastors around him continued to massage his limbs and neck. My father-in-law joined them and started pinching him, hoping that he would respond to the pain. I admired these people because, in all honesty, my husband's body smelled like mortuary chemicals.

Hope began to wane, when for a long time after he started breathing, there was no other muscular movement. He remained stiff, prompting some people to suggest that he be taken to the hospital for continuation of the recovery process. I vehemently rejected that suggestion. I strongly believed that God would finish the miracle he had gracefully begun.

However, as time passed, I noticed a gradual loss of concentration among many people, some of whom started leaving the hall. Then, it happened! My husband opened his eyes and jumped from where he lay into the arms of a rather fat Pastor Onyeka. With the support of his fellow pastors, they sat my husband in a chair. His eyes were open but dim, as he gradually adjusted to his new environment. The time was a few minutes past 5:00 p.m.

As they called me to come and greet him, I heard him speak his first few words.

"My file, my file. Where is my file?" he asked, looking a little dazed. He was later given water and tea, which he drank slowly.

The ensuing euphoria over my husband's restoration to life was so loud, and the surge of ecstatic people into the hall was so large that he had to be taken quickly into the church sanctuary. He was seated on a chair on the platform, where a mass of people watched him recover gradually. To my delight and relief, they sang praises of God; praise songs so invigorating that I couldn't help but join them. My hidden fear of having to live with a man who had been raised from the dead quickly dissolved into joy. However, the man who had inspired my faith, Evangelist Bonnke, had already left to catch a flight to Lagos. Although I later heard he had prayed in the auditorium for my husband when they were told about the arrival of a dead body, Bonnke never actually set eyes on him.

After another round of prayers to stabilise him, we finally went home to Osuma, already electrified by the news. Even in the presence of over 100 church members, neighbors, and admirers, I noticed that he still wasn't fully aware of his environment.

At dinner, he refused to eat any solid food. Instead, he opted for corn porridge and water. All the while, he complained about muscular pain. He requested a water massage in the presence of close church members, including the chairman who had argued with my father-in-law the day after my husband died.

All the while, he stared at us and wondered aloud why people were asking him so many questions. However, before we went to bed at about 8:00 p.m., he regained full consciousness and spoke coherently. In all honesty, I still felt a lingering fear when we went to sleep. In the past I didn't allow any space between us in bed. However, that night, I lay my son between us. Fear of his return to the land of the dead developed into insomnia.

I watched him all night. He prayed and slept a little. However, he soon woke up and sat on the bed for a long time. During the entire period, I continued to watch him, until he finally lay down and slept again.

At daybreak, he appeared well again, the dear husband I had married almost five years earlier. After his shower, I hugged him hard to confirm he was real.

Barely three days into my new life, I was able to weave the different experiences of the two worlds into a reality that again reminded me of God's love. I knew I was a new Dan Ekechukwu, high on the anointing and with a special mission. On the night of my recovery, a man confined to a wheel chair had been miraculously healed when he heard the news.

The physical confirmation of the enriched anointing came on the following Sunday. My church overflowed with worshippers and seats had to be rented so people could sit in the open. The Glory of God glowed so brightly that I was totally humbled.

I noticed a continuous increase in the number of worshippers at the church on subsequent Sundays. Some people even decided to attend my church early before returning to their respective churches. However, with time, I remembered that I was obeying the orders I had received in Heaven. I realized that sooner or later the voice that had first called me would speak again.

After service one afternoon, the voice reappeared. "What else must I do for you to move on, to leave this church? The message you brought from the dead—the new message I gave you—is for the Church of Jesus Christ. This is a message to be preached all over the world, not just at one location. Sinners should repent and turn to God because Heaven and hell are real."

"Yes, my Lord. I will do exactly as you requested," I exclaimed loudly. I proceeded to commit myself to a plan that would free me to travel the world.

By the following Sunday, I had invited a number of pastors from all over Onitsha to preach for ten minutes each. After they had all taken their turn, I preached my valedictory sermon and broke the news that I was leaving the church to embark on evangelism worldwide. From that day forward, I have been doing exactly what I was privileged to return to Earth to do—to spread the Voice of the Dead International Evangelism.

Quotes from Some Key Witnesses

St. Charles Borromeo's Hospital, Onitsha

We cannot comment on the resurrection of Dan Eke, because according to our records, the patient was discharged from this hospital against medical advice. The wife was forced to sign an agreement that it was her decision to move the patient out. Because of this, we cannot comment.

Pastor Oyibo Okechukwu (Dan's First Pastor)

Yes, there is no doubt that he died. I have noticed a distinct difference in him and his ministry since he was raised from the dead. Dan has really changed. If this man who attended my church in those days can become like the man he is today, we can only give glory to God.

Mrs. Mabel Ekechukwu (Dan's Mother)
I remember how he used to kick me in the womb. I always felt he was going to be special—a special person. It's the reason why out of all my children, he was the only one I took a childhood photograph of. But he turned out to be very sickly as a child. We had given up on his chance of survival, until the Iyke miracle.

Mr. Barlington Manu (Mortician)
I would say it was a stubborn corpse. It rejected most of my treatment, but surprisingly, did not decompose. From the very first day we took it in, we heard hymns throughout the night. Each time I entered the morgue, the singing stopped. When I tried to return to my room, the singing would start all over again. I had to warn the family to remove the corpse from my morgue, or I would have to deal with it with my special power [charms]. Dan Eke's body was disturbing my peace of mind.